Praise for *Flow Violento*

Scott Hulet has always possessed the ability, in conversation and in print, to make me laugh and make me think about the most important aspects of being a surfer. In Hulet World, it's about the journey and the destination, pretty much in equal measure. That's what makes his work glitter so intensely with diamonds hiding in the rough.

—Phil Jarratt, author of *Mr. Sunset* **and** *That Summer at Boomerang*, **former editor of** *Tracks* **and** *Australian Playboy*

Longtime surfer and gifted author Scott Hulet has for decades incisively read not only waves but human character. Describing being yet once more on the road in Baja California with "sparse jailhouse Spanish," he's clear-eyed, words razor-sharp and playfully hyper-idiomatic. Nor is he tempted to exempt himself from what we're all part of and party to in a world so rapidly transformed. This cumulative saga of surf and fishing safaris is at once undeceived and a song of love.

—Thomas Farber, author of *The Face of the Deep* **and** *Acting My Age*

When I read Hulet—when I slide into his groove, his take on whatever aspect of the surfing world his attention targets—I get the delightful echo of Craig Stecyk, an earlier generation's sage "watcher" over our little world, asking sometimes embarrassing questions, letting us know that he knows when we're not speaking the truth. It's the perception of a more honest voice, which can cause us to question our own, that invites us all to speak more honestly, more truly.

—Drew Kampion, author of *The Lost Coast* **and** *Dora Lives*, **former editor of** *Surfer* **magazine**

Flow Violento is haunted, in the author's own words, by the "ghosts of capers past." These ghosts are generous in bearing and rich in literary treasures. They invoke the kind of delicious nostalgia that summons our own adventurous spirits and impels us to paddle into the wild whorl of life. Hulet transcends surf writing, and this collection serves as a cartography mapped by those tracking the past, present, and future of the eternal muse. It belongs on the shelf next to *Barbarian Days* for anyone interested in riding shotgun with a keen observer of, and willing participant in, life's most memorable swells.

—**Joe Donnelly, author of** *L.A. Man* **and** *So Cal*, **editor of** *Red Canary Magazine*

Hulet takes us behind Latin America's tourist curtain, masterfully revealing the human sides of waterfront culture in Mexico, Cuba, Peru, Ecuador, and elsewhere. He does not just tell us about the sometimes-uncomfortable admixture of tradition and global change, he shows us. Much more than journalism or reportage, *Flow Violento* is a series of eloquent, heartfelt, fly-on-the-wall dispatches from a writer who has spent more than 50 years in these regions.

—**Peter Maguire, author** *Thai Stick* **and** *Breathe: A Life in Flow*

Scott Hulet's *Flow Violento* is a lavishly entertaining account of surfing that rises above mere realism and soars into sheer lunacy. His prose, which can be best described as surf chic and which gives far too much credit to this dying and shriveled culture, is lush and rarely missteps. Hulet's gift is his ability to view surfing with real ecstasy.

—**Derek Rielly, author of** *Wednesdays with Bob* **and** *Gulpilil*, **cofounder of** *BeachGrit*

Hulet has been crafting A-grade surf prose for three decades. He's relentlessly intelligent, eternally stoked, and his love for the subject matter is matched by his love of delivering it to the page with humor and grace.

—**Matt Warshaw, author of** *The Encyclopedia of Surfing* **and** *The History of Surfing*, **former editor of** *Surfer* **magazine**

To cut straight to the chase: Scott Hulet can write. And he has lived. These two facts alone make this collection of ripping saltwater yarns worth your time. The minimalist style, not a word out of place, and legitimate adventures inhabited by great characters will have you pulling out marine charts, scanning weather maps, making excuses to bosses, partners, family, and plotting your next adventure.
—**Tim Baker, author of** *Occy* **and** *Bustin' Down the Door*, **former editor of** *Tracks* **and** *Australia's Surfing Life*

Hulet's south-of-the-border reports are a masterful blend of id, ego, and super-ego. He's at the center of things, but he's a fly on the wall. He writes from the POV of the gringo, but his gringo-ness does not shape the story. It's easy to imagine the narco placing his hand on Scott's shoulder and saying, "You're one of us." And likewise the Guardia Nacional. And likewise the mariachi. And likewise the red rose peddler. And likewise the on-the-run tube junkie. Lyrical, witty, insightful, incessantly curious—Hulet's a machete-slasher of the highest order.
—**Jamie Brisick, author of** *Becoming Westerly* **and** *Have Board, Will Travel*, **former editor of** *Surfing* **magazine**

Factual information: In La Habana Vieja at El Floridita, La Cuna Del Daiquiri, we found Scott Hulet's name scrawled on the wall of tribute. This was Ernesto's favorite bar. That pretty much tells you all you need to know.
—**CR Stecyk, author of** *DogTown: The Legend of the Z-Boys*

At the end of this book, I felt like I'd just returned from a month-long trip to Baja in a beater truck: surfed-out, salt-caked, sunburned, scarred, and oh-so-very stoked.
— **Steve Hawk, former editor of** *Surfer* **magazine**

As compelling and nuanced as another slide down the sandbar, Hulet's stories are rarified, funky, and true.
—**Kimball Taylor, author of** *The Coyote's Bicycle: The Untold Story of Seven Thousand Bicycles and the Rise of a Borderland Empire*

THE SURFER'S JOURNAL

© 2024 by Journal Concepts, Inc.

All rights reserved.

Printed in China.

The Surfer's Journal
191 Avenida La Pata
San Clemente, CA
92673

surfersjournal.com

ISBN: 979-8-218-38156-1

Dust jacket artwork by Joaquin Salim
Dust jacket photograph, front left, by Dmitri Kessel/
The LIFE Picture Collection/Shutterstock
Dust jacket photograph, front right, by Abisai Morales
Dust jacket photograph, back, by Mark Kronemeyer
Author portrait by Ben Steele
Hardcover, interior, and chapter illustrations by Luis Safah

THE SURFER'S JOURNAL

For Debbie

Foreword
by Alex Wilson
   8

Introduction
by Scott Hulet
   16

Tranquila La Plaza
For a hundred or so local surfers, day tripping Sinaloa is—tentatively—back on the table.
   22

Baja Incognita
Back East, they have therapy. Out West, we have Baja.
   30

It Must Have the Smoke
Interview: Javier Plascencia.
   52

Windows on Peru
Coca drip, beef heart, and leg-quaking lefts.
   61

The Peace
A visit to Isla Cerralvo.
   69

Night and the Iguana
If you have designs on surfing—or escaping from—a prison island, you're going to have to pay.
75

Isla de Cedros: An Abecedarian Handbook
87

Finisterra
Drunk and disorderly in its modern iteration, Cabo San Lucas is a tough place to love. Divorce Beach remains its most dangerous addiction.
97

26.56.96: A Basque Continuum
103

The Other Sea of Cortez
Spare a thought for Sonora.
108

Sucker-Free on the Ruta del Sol
Just say the words and we'll beat the birds down to Acapulco Bay.
116

Off the Arroyo
Alonso Macklis traces his lineage to the days of sail. Join him for a day in his hometown of La Ribera.
122

The Setenta-Mineral
131

Our Man in the Antilles
Chris Klopf shoots the Dominican Republic.
134

Reefed
An unsung Baja harbor offers quick access for a land-based hit to Sacramento Reef.
143

Stackin' 'Em
Kelly Catian y Familia de San Quintín.
151

Café Racer
Miguel Tudela pins it through greater Lima's surf culture.
160

En Baja
A recent John Comer show in San Jose del Cabo, Baja Sur, Mexico.
170

Riding Cowgirl
Off the East Cape on *Vaquera*.
175

Punta Impresario
Israel Preciado is driven by his Punta Mita beginnings—and an improbably detailed account of a midnight border crossing.
183

The Mangroves of Topolobampo
Fishing the estuaries of Sinaloa with Lupe López.
191

Mr. Mayor, the Floor is Yours
Interview: Serge Dedina.
199

Tentative in Manabí
A flâneur's search for a lid—and sand-sucking drainers—in Ecuador.
209

El Molino Viejo (The Old Mill)
San Quintín, BCN.
218

AKA Stoner's
How the original secret spot was overshadowed by time and inclination.
221

Two Dog Circus
Surrealismo in central Baja.
231

Acknowledgments
238

Foreword

I was in a desert, camped on an empty point, when I first registered on one of the global antenna arrays monitored by Scott Hulet. He was looking for someone who might be interested in applying for an underling position at *The Surfer's Journal*, where he was the editor, and across oceans and desolation he'd somehow become aware of exactly where the group I'd been traveling with was located, exactly when we were scheduled to pop back on the grid, the rough sketches of my resume as a writer/editor (whatever those were worth), and the contact information required to send me a short electronic missive, just as we were passing out of comms again, suggesting that, should I ever return to California, he'd like to have a conversation.

My group drove past a minefield later that day and, other than violent death, the thing I found myself most concerned with was what he'd think of my nonresponse to his email, since it would be at least another week before I'd be able to RSVP in the positive. Of course, he also somehow knew the rest of my itinerary, so it was pointless to worry.

I drove from San Diego up to *TSJ* HQ in San Clemente on my second afternoon back in the US, ostensibly, to interview with him. He met me at the door to the office and, instead of ushering me into some kind of formal question and answer session about my credentials, he promptly led me back out to the parking lot.

Soon we were bombing down the hill in his truck toward the ocean, talking about travel, food, books, surf, fish, photos, coastal San Diego, non-coastal San Diego, Montauk, New York City, Mexico City, Oaxaca, et cetera. I downloaded the report from my trip, and he asked a series of cagey, geolocational questions that indicated he knew more about where I'd been than I did. We ate braised tongue tacos at the Buena Vista Market in Dana Point, where he ordered for both of us in Spanish. On the way back up the hill, he packed a dip and asked me to send over some writing samples.

Debriefing later with my wife, sweating over the pieces I'd forwarded, I told her my first impression was of someone literary, hyper intelligent, and loquacious, with a sense of mischief and a vocabulary that can leave you running for either the *Urban Dictionary* or a thesaurus. I'd of course been reading *The Surfer's Journal* since I was a teenager, and I knew his writing and editing, and I obviously desperately wanted the job, but now I also kind of just wanted another excuse to go hang out with him.

There must have been something halfway resembling merit in whatever I'd said during lunch or sent in my samples, because I was invited up for a subsequent visit. This time we ate lamb birria with consommé and further established a shared interest in jellied bone marrow served over sopes, self-indulgence, desert noir by the likes of Cormac McCarthy, sea fiction by Peter Matthiessen, and thin-lipped, down-the-line point waves.

Hulet seemed to particularly like that I knew who Robert Stone was, and that we agreed *Dog Soldiers* was his best novel.

He was a little suspicious that I hadn't read any James Salter and didn't own a single-fin (both since remedied several times over), but was heartened by the knowledge that my dad used to moonlight as a commercial clam digger, which dovetailed with his own more-pelagic fishing obsessions.

It was enough, anyway, for him to offer me a desk and introduce me to the rest of the edit team. Since then we've made thousands of magazine pages together, a process during which he's taught me to liberally apply topspin in both ping-pong and caption writing, how to sight-cast for halibut, and the value of things like an overly long brunch (lox Benedict), which, stretching into the afternoon, may appear completely unproductive but, when viewed properly, provides exactly the frame of mind and nutritive ballast required to kill a deadline.

He's also literally handed over maps and charts—after vetting my abilities to compartmentalize and obfuscate among those not to be trusted—scribbled with decades of knowledge, detailing everything from the tide mechanics of dusty, wrapping coves to how to effectively run a vaunted magazine. Somewhere along the way I learned the backstory of why his OG pals call him "Mace," a misadventure that, predictably, involves a can of mace and a very well-known biker gang. It's been an education and a pastime.

Reading the travel pieces in this collection with the hindsight of those lessons, 26 stories assembled from Hulet's decades of bouncing through Mexico and across other points in Latin America, excursions spent fishing, surfing, eating, reporting, and running his general flâneur's operations, I was struck by how much his work evokes his actual character. His black humor, his reporter's eye, his literary underpinnings, his mischievous id and inner gremlins, his affinity for oddities, his deep understanding of and curiosity for people and places, the research he does on the ground and in the stacks before and after a trip—it's all here, so much so that these pages almost perfectly mimic the experience of having him riding shotgun, noting waypoints, as you speed along through the desert:

See that restaurant? It has the best *guisados* on the peninsula. See that ranch? The owner used to herd his cattle in a '74 Monte Carlo. See the grass from the rains? Locally, and in Sinaloa, it's called zacate. A forest of cardon is a *cardonal*. Yuccas, a *yuccatal*. Wild onions grow over that ridge. There're petroglyphs back there, up the arroyo. One depicts a Spanish galleon. Those mountains are shot through with mining shafts. This point was once a Cochimí encampment. You can still find their abalone shells in the sand dunes. Read Homer Aschmann's *Ethnography of Baja California*. Turn here. Take the left-hand fork west of the volunteer palm. Follow it until you get to the salt flats. What? You want to know the translation for jack rabbit? It's *liebre*, Spanish for stringy, oily vermin.

Of course, an author's writing is always a reflection of the mind behind the keyboard, but the result in most final texts is also, generally, just a cypher or a mask that conveys an approximation, an effect of a person, rather than a truly accurate representation of their being. It's exceedingly rare to meet an author who appears in three dimensions in their work, especially through travel writing. This book, though, is like Hulet distilled—a high-proof spirit of his voice delivering insider wisdoms, guidance, points of interest, jokes, and observations.

In a lot of ways, it falls into the yarn-spinning lineage at *The Surfer's Journal*, where he's spent nearly 25 years collaborating with

Steve Pezman, another writer whose stories, with their warmth and sense of fun in recounting his minor scrapes and hustles for free food, cheap beer, and empty waves, equally encapsulate and evoke his actual presence. I like to think this symbiosis is why they've worked so well together for so long, producing so much great work, so consistently. They've oriented their writing, editing, and essentially their lives around shared reference points and appreciations.

Hulet and I were somewhere south of El Rosario recently, about a decade after that first email he sent me. The road had opened up and we were skimming over the central plateau, watching the light turn pink across the granite hoodoos and the first stands of cirios. I was concentrating on weaving around the craters in the pavement, a series of alignment-jarring bomb holes left by a recent chubasco. We were doing a steady 75 mph, on pace to make our final waypoint before nightfall. We'd loaded firewood in Maneadero, block ice, fresh cilantro, and cases of beer at the last market, and now the truck was fully provisioned for the backcountry, oversteering a touch whenever its center of gravity shifted.

The radio was off and Hulet and I hadn't spoken in maybe an hour. We'd both just cleared a deadline (without Benedicts) and needed the silence. As the day had extended toward dusk, in fact, our communications had fallen from senseless jabbering into a form of atavistic gestures, used only to point out the occasional landmark or a potential hazard. We were experiencing the familiar peeling effect of Baja: Drive south, away from the matrix, until the land empties, and you can feel the layers of stress flayed away, replaced by the stillness and the expanses of the desert.

Our stomachs were still processing enough *adobada* from Hulet's favorite roadside attraction that the timing of some sort of gaseous violence was entirely plausible. In hindsight, I should have known something was afoot, but my attention was focused on the road, like I mentioned.

The first rip was short and high pitched, more of a preliminary rangefinder than an opening salvo. Hulet even cracked the window, without comment, to sell its authenticity. (Something I've realized from spending time around writers, especially good ones, is that even off the page they understand the suspension of disbelief rests in applied detail.)

He waited until the air had flushed the cab before closing the window, then unloaded a second and third series of long, ragged undulations that evoked a tearing sound, like someone shredding apart thick sheafs of fabric. This went on intermittently until we made our next scheduled pitstop to top off with the fuel pirates in Cataviña.

Climbing out of the truck in the half-light, he shook his head, cocked his lower back at a pained and contorted angle—which indicated any further movement in any direction, even if toward salvation, might result in his undoing—and unleashed another round of concussions.

"You're not right," I said. "If you can't make it to a toilet, I'm going to go find you a bucket."

That's when he opened his palm to reveal the real source of the commotion—not a whoopee cushion, which would have been way too obvious and pedestrian. The device, instead, was some sort of mini rubberized bellows, a gag item that, clearly, could be manipulated for all manner of pitches and durations of varying impact. I think he got it somewhere in Tijuana, in roughly the same warrens of the city he used to frequent with his dad to buy switchblades and jumping beans in the late 1960s.

I've since learned it's a standard-issue article in his dopp kit, even if he rarely deploys it. I've often wondered if his grandfather, who according to family lore worked for the OSS in Indonesia around mid-century, would have packed something similar for his own field excursions. (Given the bloodline: probably.)

An hour later, Hulet was posted up reading a story collection by one of the Russians, eating sliced tomatoes topped with cotija, vinegar, olive oil, basil, capers, and sipping a nice *cristalino*. If each of us contains multitudes, the high/low culture within him clearly runs across a much vaster chasm than the average.

It's this dichotomy that makes his writing so much fun to read and the point of view he conveys so compelling. He takes it all seriously—but not too seriously, another lesson he's taught me. Like all surfers (and writers), he understands the value of making something that's exceedingly difficult look exceedingly easy.

There are isolated sentences and even minor clauses throughout in this collection, conveying some sort of insight or knowledge, that only exist because they're backed by a whole iceberg of experience hidden under the surface—thousands of hours spent fixing flat tires, losing fish at the rail, and exploring back alleys and two-tracks. So read it attuned for subtext. Or read it recklessly, carried along by speed and momentum. In either case, you'll be enjoying these stories as their author intended.

—*Alex Wilson*

Introduction

Flying into La Habana at noon, the Caribbean wraps the island in a warm *abrazo*. That bright field of blue resolves into high def until you can see the sea's pores—white horses rough sanded by the midday trades. A dazzling, jewel-toned cerulean and the tobacco brown of Cuba herself. A baroque and regal palette.

But I prefer to arrive at night. Havana appears not like the furiously lit cymbal crash of Mexico City or New York, but as a flickering, amber-colored apparition. The low-voltage, Soviet-era lights of the city struggle against greater odds. From experience, I know that I'll have two hours to shed my skin. My driver will stop at a dark doorway to magically turn 500 dollars into a brick of CUP, the nearly valueless national currency. I'll check into the casa just long enough to stash my phone and Mac in the safe and change my shirt. Then it's straight to La Zorra y El Cuervo, the treasured jazz cavern in Vedado, for the second set.

I count more and more on such rituals. After a traumatic brain injury in 2018—*un infarto cerebral*—I've become beholden to tradition. Another side effect of having your eggs vigorously scrambled is that your emotions are closer to the surface. Music kind of makes me tear up. I've also become less garrulous than my friends remember. My aphasia makes me self-conscious, especially when speaking Spanish. The condition robbed me of my ability to roll my Rs, which pisses me off to no end. But make your weakness your strength, they say. My speech therapist gave me a Spanish-language DMV manual to recite to her, bless her heart. A lifelong writer's infatuation with idioms has made me a trafficker in slang. My driver knows this. I tell him to drop me off, that I'll *darle una pierna*. (Cubans say they'll "give it the leg.")

Slang can open doors, but it can also lead to false starts. In the aspirationally named VIP Lounge at Rodriguez International in Tijuana (my hub and portal to all things LatAm), a young lady from Monterrey overheard me order from the barman. I'd merely caught his attention by raising my voice and calling him *joven*. Assuming fluency, she pointed out a woman standing in the doorway. From the hundred words she rapidly spoke, I only really grasped her clucking, "*Corrida sin aceite*." Running without oil? I couldn't hear any rattling valves, but I'm no mechanic. Context helped. The woman in the doorway looked wrung out and hungover. *Bien crudo*. But she also caught the eye of everyone in the lounge. Severely parted black hair. Threaded eyebrows. Bejeweled, caviar-spoon nails. An invisible Colombian girdle garroting her torso, amplifying her monumental principal asset. In short, a Culichi, a product of ranch town beauty pageants, telenovelas, and everything else springing from the city of Culiacán. "*Culichi Culichi*," the children sing, "*mucha nalga poca chichi*." She teetered into the room, her floral wrap dress straining its pinnings, her heels clicking on the tile like rifle rounds being chambered into a brush gun. "*Si si si*," I admitted to my barmate. "*Obvio. Bien Culichi.*" I turned back to my papaya and *cortado* breakfast, keeping an eye on the flight toteboard.

The bulk of the stories in this book originate from that very airport. My Mexican Turismo account affords me an annual airline pass, which I abuse to no end. Articles, both assigned and self-generated, find me supplying magazine clients, principally *The Surfer's Journal*, but some saltwater fishing journals as well. Other times I find myself going on a lark. Guadalajara for the book fair and to see the Orozco murals. Dipping into Nayarit for point-wave therapy. Checking in at Lima's Club Waikiki, where a pisco sour is invariably shoved into my claw upon entry. Week-long trips to cities I know nothing about, disappearing solo (always solo), down to the waterfront for news of the weather, the birds, and the bait.

It wasn't always thus. For 20-some years I sat in the corner office of a surf magazine, dutifully building run sheets, lunching with writers and photographers, and more or less melting away. Sure, I still surfed a few days a week locally and never missed a winter minus-tide cycle down in the central Baja zone I call the "Lesser Shag." But surfing was becoming an itchy phantom limb. The flip side of making your love your 24/7 vocation is that the all-consuming nature of the chosen topic fills you up in such a way that the act itself can become redundant. *La vida putería*, I suppose. Until. Until the sea spray charges your lungs. Until you lock into full-body trim whomping a shorebreak tube. Until you see a pelican wisely stall for an encroaching section. Then you remember. The crawl back into service is arduous. (Great Christ, where did my trapezius go?) But crawl you must. Avert your eyes. For both of our sakes.

I wasn't believing in the very idea of this volume, of this exercise. The idea of another surf book, more surfing stories, more surf "content," further additions to the groaning and overburdened bridge of it all, gave me pause. But focusing on my beloved Mexico and other points in Latin America—the places that inform, that haunt, that sustain all of my lifelong love for the nearshore life—gave me a hook I could believe in.

The surfers and fishermen I've run with make horrible tourists. They travel with intent. The more interesting among them also voyage with curiosity, historical and literary references, and a startling sense of geography. It's unspoken on the beach or at the rail, but you recognize it in their choices. Their itineraries. Their books. Their boards and their tackle. The way they disappear into the city, alone or paired up, once ashore.

Back at La Zorra y El Cuervo, the pianist closes out the sublime, waltz-timed Eddie Harris number "Essence of Matter." Predictably, I get something caught in my eye. Dude on my left sees me and nods, as if to say he gets it. Looking to the piano man with his bloodshot eyes, he says, "*Ese hombre tiene flow… flow violento.*"

—*Scott Hulet*

Tranquila La Plaza

For a hundred or so local surfers, day tripping Sinaloa is—tentatively—back on the table.

From *The Surfer's Journal*, Volume 29, Number 1, 2020

We're running up the coast in gray light. First waypoint: the tollbooth burritos at El Mármol. Tollbooth burritos are a Sinaloan specialty in a land of specialties. The state is revered for its cuisine. *Aguachile negro, ceviche de sierra, callo de hacha, robalo zarandeado.* All of the joy, all of the art, all of the beautiful Spanish euphony of the local seafood preparation is matched by the gifts of the land. The grass-fed beef, the wild chiltepin chiles, tomatoes so luridly plump and curvaceous that the local Pacific League ball club is called the Tomato Farmers. That horn of plenty is funneled right into the humble roadside burrito, five for three bucks, including a *cafécito.*

Sinaloa is Mexico's grocery store. The pharmacy, on the other hand, is up the coastal plain in the Sierra Madre Occidental. It's been that way since the first Chinese laborers planted poppies in the days of Porfirio Díaz. Food and meds. Vons and Sav-on. Everybody knows it. No use in hiding it. Opium gum and weed, now synthetics. Rivers of slivers, all heading north. It's complicated. Complicated enough that the proceeds end up goosing our 401(k)s. There should be Wall Street bankers locked up in supermax, blow-drying Chapo's socks. But let's talk surfing.

The light turns a nicotine yellow and we've got the pedal down, making tracks before the devil makes wind. Our caravan comprises three cars, two Sinaloan photographers, two national rippers, and two half-time Mexicans—Skip McCullough and yours truly. We're on the spoor, snouts to the ground, hunting rifled sand cones.

The swells surge up the eastern Mar de Cortés in patterns defined by their angle of access. When entering the Sea's mouth from an appropriate window, their repeated passage carves out cusps and scallops, pushing sand north to the next headland. You see their flexing backs from high spots on the road.

The sun's rays skylight the sierra. We stick out like boar teats with our racked boards. This is a district where it pays to have your hackles pricked, your ears to the ground, and, from David Mamet's *Spartan*, your motherfuckers set to "receive." In the dicier parts of rural Mexico, situational awareness is an art. It's having eyes in the back of your head while appearing nonchalant, like you don't care what befalls you. This attitude will provide some window of escape should fate come knocking, the sort of surprise defense relied on by hedgehogs and pufferfish. An "only hope" type of thing. Our crew performs the most natural human response to uneasiness: nervous laughter.

Things are generally cool right now. The Sinaloa Cartel maintains an impregnable grasp on its home state. The plaza, as they say, is calm. The local government likes it this way. Furthermore, following the mysterious murder of two Australian surfers in 2015, the authorities (and here that includes the extrajudicial) have issued a tacit "don't dick with *turismo*" edict. I know this is true because a *taxi libre* driver told me, waving away my concerns like flies. The murders brought heat to the plaza. Bad for business. When this happens, some usual suspects are rounded up, mineral-watered into a confession, and dog-walked off to crime college.

For now, locals say, the carjackings, kidnappings, and sundry banditry have backed down. People are seen smiling as they drive Mex 15, not squeezing the wheel and bracing for evasive maneuvers. One no longer feels like a misery tourist here, blithely averting their gaze from some atrocity visited on the populace. Besides, we're on the beach, not up in Culiacán, that Versailles of *narcocultura*. Famous throughout the land. Personal zoos. Narco juniors cashing out Lambo Huracánes from Fendi man purses. Ocelot hat bands. Air-conditioned marble crypts. Ass implants.

Here on the coast, one can play the margins. There's some brinkmanship involved, but it's a far cry from recent memory. The local surfers feel it. Rodrigo Arregui, a surfer from down the coast in Mazatlán, confirms. "We have had difficult times," he says. "But now it's just like anywhere in the world. You don't get in trouble if you're not messing up."

Rodrigo is riding with us this morning. He works this area's waves like it's his job. Local surfers from Culiacán to Mazatlán are once again day tripping the handful of quality spots dotting the coast along the southern Los Mochis bight. One of the top surfers from his town, Rodrigo looks at such road trips the way that we all do. They offer hits of discovery. A respite from the mundane. Waves beyond the normal pale. But in Sinaloa—especially in Sinaloa—there are no promises. That goes double for gringos.

We stand out. It's nothing racial. But profiling makes for efficient, if imperfect, security. Outside the obvious tourism zones, a gringo traveling through Sinaloa is an inscrutable and unwelcome presence. Those in the funny business will make you as a narc, a spook, a rat—or all of the above.

As a US citizen, our government makes it abundantly clear: Do not go to Sinaloa. Travel Advisory Level 4. Same as Syria, Yemen, Somalia. Baja Sur and Norte clock in at Level 2. The State Department reserves the same grave language they use for straight-up war zones, adding that they may not (read: cannot and will not) help you should things jump the curb. Federal employees are not allowed anywhere near the joint.

All of which makes our trip not the best way to surf Sinaloa. At least not for Skip and me. The best way, oddly enough, might be to book a week at either Cardon Adventure Resort or Sinaloa Surf Adventures, the two regional surf camps. The travel warnings still apply, but you won't be nearly so exposed. They have left points on lock. Literally, in the case of the latter camp. Doubts? Try surfing El Patole, the coast's best pointbreak, as a non-guest. The entire headland and point are fenced off. The guard is deputized and said to keep a toaster in a shoulder holster. This isn't some egalitarian, no-one-owns-the-ocean drum circle. This is Sinaloa. There are maybe 4,000 other waves in Mexico where one can surf without such considerations. Not here.

"They don't want us locals," says Rodrigo. "It's annoying sometimes. Like, I haven't surfed El Patole for about nine years. Cardon is not too welcoming either but we find our ways, and once we are there the waves are amazing and you get to surf with the guys from the camp. Nice people most of the time!"

I am told that every need is provided for at the camps. Three gourmet-adjacent squares, cocktails, massages. You will be compounded up and limbo'd down. Nightly video playback. Trophy largemouth fishing at a local *presa*. Guest chefs. Distillery tours. Sounds nice.

Again, not our path. We're flogging it local style. My Sinaloan friends have been hounding me to visit, and they're housing us in their own grand fashion. They know my fondness for octopus and bachata, for the sincere and gracious *patas saladas* ("salty feet," slang for natives) of the Pearl of the Pacific, for the snook and the miracle of riverine jaguars in the southern esteros. The waves brought me here long, long ago and opened a cultural passageway in the way fine writing does. They didn't have to ask twice.

We pull off the toll road and into a sort of *palapa*-ville. A series of local-knowledge-only turns and we're at the bottom of a left point. Carlos Rocha, "El Mantaraya," leaps from his car and performs a sort of triple jump, landing atop a fence post. He's muscular and compact, built like a lightweight boxer or knife fighter. He's been invited to join us based on his reputation as a Phil Edwards-conjuring stylist.

Skip McCullough is on his heels. He's Windansea to the bone and our token *gabacho*. Pops has hauled him to Mexico his whole life and it shows. He has humorous and fluid use of obscure, street-level Mexican idioms. He scythes away on little Xanadu blades. There's an FU to his line choices, and one can't help but feel a synthesis of Andy, Dane, and maybe—how can this be possible?—Chris O'Rourke. He's fresh off a WQS win in the Philippines. His wallet is jammed with Philippine pesos, English pounds, millions of rupiah. There's an undeniable natural gift on display here, in both talent and roots charisma.

The drive north had Skip in a car with the Mexicans. He copped an earful of Sinaloa intel and quickly downloaded his learnings. "Chalino Sánchez is the Tupac of Mexican culture," Skip says. "Rodrigo, Mantaraya, and I had Chalino bumping at full volume the whole ride. They told me if you don't listen to Chalino Sánchez while you're in Sinaloa…well, did you even go to Sinaloa?"

Rodrigo joins us on the berm and spits knowledge. It's good, he says, even for here. Overhead, glassy, and unabated. He and Skip seem properly mounted with low-fat, Formula 1 thrusters. It's barreling, after all. Carlos, on the other hand, is dragging a heavy 9'6" single-fin down the beach by the nose. Just a man, some trunks, and a board. Our *pata salada*, Rodrigo is economical and accomplished. Skip carves in a way that should have some much higher-profile Californians checking their swagger. But Carlos blew all of us out. He proved inventive, was a dervish paddler, and displayed such style that you cursed your lesser blessings. He made mince out of the challenging longshore sweep, catching 30 waves an hour. That's including a couple of long bodysurfs chasing his leashless board. It was uncanny. Dude's *suavecito* to the nth.

The success of the day's score has us cackling on the run back to town. It's midday and all is well. There are cars on the road. No sketchy *halcone* lurkers giving us the once over. Not a surfer in sight. We make plans to repeat on the morrow.

Two days later and the winds change. Rodrigo suggests heading south to a deep-water harbor entrance. It's one of his home breaks and he's amped, both at the conditions and the chance to share a spot with his new clique. A short hike is involved. Rounding the corner, we find two spongers out enjoying the proceedings. And by that, I mean getting relentlessly, serially pitted. The wave? In a nutshell, it looks like a short piece of Honolua Bay grafted with Salsipuedes. Too generous? I'll flip to Skip, who surfs for his bread:

"What an incredible wave. If you have heard anything about surf in Sinaloa, you've heard about this place. The wave *barrels*. And I learned that the water is always way colder out there. I'm glad as hell I had a wetsuit jacket.

"Ardilla [Rodrigo is known locally as "Chipmunk"] is a super-technical surfer who knows exactly which waves to go on. He would wait and wait, but he was always on the best waves. Mantaraya, though, dude doesn't give a fuck. No cord. He was taking off and surfing like he had a brand-new leash. He would do turns, walk the nose, pull in. It didn't matter that he wasn't connected to his board. He lost it a couple times, basically demolished it. In a hasty scramble, we found a guy who could crudely fix it that afternoon. The next day, on a heavy first wave, Carlos lost it on the rocks again. Young guy, old school. Just part of the game for him."

We called Skip out for dancing on the rocks, clutching his nuts, and howling, "That waves spit 11 times!" He stared us down, rounded up, and made it an even dozen.

We celebrated over pizza in a converted boatyard. Rodrigo and Carlos fist-knocked their fortune. We knew what they were on about. This was a pregnant pause. A time wrinkle in US/Latin policy. For a variety of reasons, ranging from privatization to fear to State Department no-fly proclamations, non-surf-camp Americans from the other side had more or less ceased surfing here. Crowd-wise, one could hear a pin drop. We saw virtually no other surfers. The locals, such as they are, are infrequent visitors. The peak-swell days get ridden, but there's plenty meat left on the bone.

Hailing as he does from a surf town of millions, Skip was dumbfounded. "I've been two hours from a south-swell, sand-point heaven and didn't even know it."

Rodrigo assured us the situation could turn on a dime. For now, the vibe was a sort of hushed gratitude. One gets the feeling that there's a lot of that going on in coastal Sinaloa.

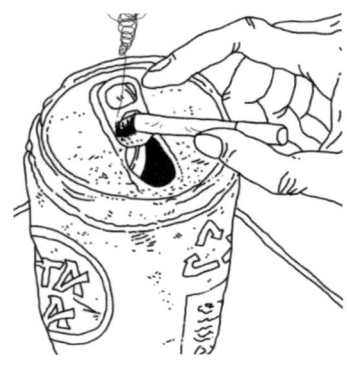

Baja Incognita

On a recent run down Cabras way, it dawned on me. Four generations of men in my line had regularly dropped into Baja. On a spoken level, it was for the fish, the light, and the pliancy of time. All legit reasons, those, but I've only just realized what the real motivation was. Back East, they have therapy. Out West, we have Baja.

From *Longboard Quarterly*, Volume 3, Number 4, 1995

"It's not the beer cans littering the side of the road that are tragic. It's the road itself."

—*Edward Abbey*

DISCLAIMER

No entran moscas en boca cerrada.
Flies can't enter a closed mouth.

The point was shat upon by the surf media in the '70s, rat eaten in the '80s, and finally buried in a '90s feature article. There are now restaurants, air tours, a namesake clothing company, development plans, and rather clear retribution jihads for several journalists.

It doesn't take a Rhodes Scholar to realize that Baja could crumble under the weight of the Californian surfing populace. Many feel that every magazine writer who names names, draws maps, and throws clues should be drummed out of the inner circle, relieved of their inflatable velour camp mattresses, and banished to their anemic little home breaks. We couldn't agree more. Hell, even the lower mammals keep their nests clean.

We've been wanting to do a Baja feature, but were only interested in doing it right. No names. *Incognita*. Additionally, all reasonable precautions have been taken in the photo-editing process, with particular care given to cropping out telltale headlands and other obvious landmarks where underground locales are used.

However, for the few among you searching for a guidebook, a shortcut, a dilution of the experience in exchange for expediency, let's cut to the chase. We're going to feed you three absolute Baja secret spots, spelled right out with their mapped, designated names. Break out your highlighters.

1) Punta Chivato. Halfway into the gulf, this left point comes alive twice a decade for an hour or so when a 175-degree chubasco blows right up the chute. Mark your calendar.

2) Roso's. Surreptitiously located in front of the Rosarito Beach Hotel. Interesting left-predominate peaks during souths. Future surf camp? Ask your financial advisor.

3) Punta Bandera, aka Bola de Cagada. Adjacent to the emergency sewer outfall between Punta Bandera and San Antonio del Mar. Bring your dental floss.

TO COME OF AGE IN A DRY PLACE

One of my earliest memories finds me posing for a snapshot on my mother's shoulders, who is in turn atop my father's. We're on the bluffs at Campo Lopez, and there's a fat blanket of June gloom overhead. The photo was probably being composed by Grandpa Joe-Joe, and it's probable that great-granddad "Pop" Mayes is lurking nearby, perhaps shucking mussels. It's 1963.

Strangely, it happens that many of my crucial developmental moments occurred in Mexico: first plate of *lengua* (Ensenada, 1969); first fumblings with a female (Playa Santispac, Conception Bay, Christmas, 1975); first beer in a bar (Hermosillo, 1976); first driving lesson (Vizcaíno Desert, 1976); first dry tube ride (Baja Tradewinds, 1977); first viewing of own stomach lining (Salsipuedes, 1978); first and last night in the can (Primo Tapia, 1981). Proud moments, all, but certainly not unique. Rite-of-passage trips down Mexico 1 are pandemic in the SoCal surf crawl. Always have been. Probably always will be.

For the seasoned Baja freaks, the surf is just a paint job. Underneath lie the dark swirlings of the land itself. It remains one of this hemisphere's last barren places. Our planet is peppered with tens of thousands of tropical islands and myriad temperate wave zones, but Baja's rare merging of maritime and desert climates is found in only four other global locales. The land commands respect. When asked to describe the country's topography, Hernán Cortés crumpled up a sheet of paper and turned it in the candlelight, illustrating the parched, arroyo-ridden landscape. He couldn't have schooled his patrons better with a satellite photo. What's truly remarkable is that those same arroyos feed into larger barrancas, which in turn deliver point-building waterflow (over millennia, of course; some areas receive less than an inch of rain per annum) and the results need to be surfed to be believed.

The nature of the place is such that one long trip can provide the traveler with a quiver of good stories, but the real tales (and real waves) are the province of the journeyman alone. If someone who's only been down a dozen times tries to enlighten you, don't listen. If you're lucky enough to run into a devoted mossback, prick up your ears. At the least you'll be educated, and what he tells you might just save your skin.

> *No hay camino mas seguro que el que acaban de robar.*
> **The road that suffered the most recent robbery is the safest.**

My friend wasn't up to the drive home, so I dropped him at the airport in Loreto with the understanding that I'd deliver his truck in a week or so. This was fine by me. I'd packed an emergency road kit for just such an occasion. I unrolled the parcel and inventoried the fruits of my foresight: a bottle of Hennesey cognac, a bootlegged cassette of Patti Smith spoken word, a pound of pistachios from the stand in Miraflores, and a copy of Bowles' *The Sheltering Sky*. Further, there were several Ballenas still swimming in the cooler. I was looking solid for the run home and was making good time by dusk.

There's little in the world like night-driving solo in Baja. The threat of seven-shrine blind corners, road agents, and shit-dumb cattle are considerable factors, but by pegging it between 40 and 50 mph and being quasi-vigilant, it's more than negotiable—it's edifying.

Like a county fair spook house, scenes both haunting and comical rear up in your headlamps: An emaciated, braying donkey tangled in a range fence. An old man at midnight, pushing an ice cream cart, bells jingling, 50 miles from the nearest town. A circus trailer with blinking Christmas lights and neon murals, all mounted on a '50s Dino flatbed truck. Career Baja dream-fodder, all of these. But for me, the capper was yet to come.

I picked up the gringo hitchhiker at the Jesús y María Pemex station. He was older than me, perhaps even 30. A surfer, no less. His skin was sun blasted, his hair was long and dry as straw, and he carried all his gear stuffed in an old canvas board bag swaddling his 7'11". I tried to help him throw the whole mess into the bed, but he stepped quickly to block me. Must have weighed a ton, as he had to squat-thrust the thing onto the railing, and then see-saw it in.

As we coasted down the high-desert grade in Mexican overdrive, aka neutral, he explained that he'd been foot-camping out toward Rancho X, working over a section of shallow reef-breaks that lacked the quality (and crowds) of the name-brand point nearby.

He'd taken a Tres Estrellas bus from T-town to the junction, camped under a paloverde tree, and caught a ride with an empty ice truck out to the fish camp. From there he'd hoofed it. He went in with a hundred bucks, a portable filter/desalinator rig, a backpack full of Top Ramen, and some books. The full monk trip.

Somewhere in the Manolito bight, he found the ribs of an old Gold Rush-era coastal packet sticking out of the flats during the record minus tides. He worked the shipwreck for three days, digging and burrowing with his entrenching tool. By the end of his stay, he'd unearthed 15 pounds of hand-cast brass fittings and gold-foil detailing from the hapless vessel.

As we burned through Catavina, he said he was estimating the take at $500.

One of the mysteries of the peninsula is illustrated every time you run into old acquaintances out on the points, fellows you haven't even thought of in years. Three seasons later, I recognized him in the water at Swimming Pool Point. I was impressed when he mentioned that he'd been rummaging around Mexico for two years, and was absolutely blown away when he told me how he'd done it: The ship's antiquities had sold at Christie's for a clean $35,000.

> *Los muertos a la sepulrura, los vivos a la travesura.*
> **The dead go to the burial ground, the living keep on playing around.**

Packed and loaded for two days, we crossed at San Ysidro at three o'clock in the morning. In the moonlight, we saw north lines breaking off the rocks at La Misión, and we let off a couple of hoots. The angle was dead-set perfect for the points, and we had two weeks at our disposal.

Passing the stone frog at El Mirador at 3:55, we smoked through the road cut above Salsi's at 70 mph. The Big Sur of Mex 1 is always an eye grabber, even at night, and we strained in our seats trying to get a look down to the point.

When the stalled van appeared in the highway ahead of us, we locked up the wheels and went sideways. There was a Freightliner cab-over parked 20 feet ahead of the wreck. I jumped out of the truck and walked toward the van. It was apparent that it had rear-ended the abandoned semi at speed.

Peering around the roof pillar, I stone-cold froze when I saw a wispy-mustached teenaged face staring right back at me, grinning. The steering-wheel axle had gone clean through his chest, and every liter of blood he owned had drained onto the floorboards, leaving him deflated, colorless, and somewhat *muerto*.

"Geez, is someone in there?"

My friend's voice sounded unreasonably loud.

"Gray-boy," I answered.

He looked over my shoulder, went green, and blew.

We hopped in the truck and crawled past the vehicles. The feds would be by shortly to mop up, and neither of us wanted to be around for that.

Ten years later, when either of us catches the other taking a corner a little hot or when we're scouting a dicey arroyo crossing, a quick glance and the grim-humored utterance of "gray-boy" urges temperance.

> *Arriba ya del caballo, hay que aguantar los respingos.*
> **If you want to mount the steed, you must be prepared for the bucking.**

My gal and I were on what could accurately be described as our third date. I had called it a camping trip and mentioned that her '73 Super Beetle was eminently capable of the run to the Tip. She was unsure, but still game. (We both became People's Car zealots when, a month later, we pulled into the V-Dub dealership in Lazaro Cardenas on the mainland for a tune-up. The mechanic informed us that the Beetle was in superb running condition and required no maintenance).

In fact, the damage toll for the entire six-week venture consisted of a blown tire, compliments of the kids who seed the highway with carpet tacks a half-mile on either side of their tire-repair shop at the LA Bay junction. A foul entrepreneurial device, but *doble salud* for desert ingenuity.

Tire freshly plugged, we were making up lost time on that long, straight stretch that stripes through cardon and boojum forest, engine hatch up for cooling and windows down for breeze.

That's when the dove bombed out of the sky in a Stuka dive and neatly bisected itself on the fin of my roof-racked Yater, a mist of feathers and breast meat spackling the windshield.

We've since learned that romantic notions of road song have a habit of giving way to bloody tableaux on the Carretera Transpeninsular. Some incidents are as seemingly trite as an exploding bird. Some we view as more tragic as they involve human lives. Any way you cut it, there are places in the world where highways just don't belong.

ARCHETYPES

De médico, poeta, y loco todos tenemos un poco.
There is a little doctor, poet, and madman in all of us.

Ranger of the points, he lives in a stone house in the nook of a headland where he plants abalone, studies botany, and rides waves. Back in the States, he's artist-in-residence at an Oregon college. Here he looks after the shark fishermen camped nearby, and has instructed them in the construction of pit toilets and general sanitation. As a competent field medic, he sets bones, sews-up reef cuts, and makes sure the children stay healthy. In return, the coastal *ejido* has granted him asylum in the little cove, which fronts a consistent right point. When that right gets real, nobody takes off deeper.

Many of the fishermen are migrants from Zacatecas and Chihuahua, and they view his knowledge of the region with solemn appreciation. Under his brief tutelage, surfers too have headed home a shade more enlightened than when they arrived.

I first met him in '84, walking up the coastal track. I found it curious that a gringo would be on foot. He'd been looking after a neighbor's windmill, he said, making sure the trickle of water was being pumped to the livestock. When asked if he needed a lift, he just smiled and said he wasn't going far. He waited for us to drive a ways up the road, and I saw him turn into the brush through the rearview mirror.

Back home, the memory of this sunburnt *guero* living alone in the desert worked on me. I knew he was getting waves, and he exuded a trickster's confidence that made me want to know more about him.

The following winter I ran into him again, a bit farther up the coast. He came creeping down the single-track to our camp one evening, carefully driving his truck on the ridge route, skylining himself to telegraph his approach. Baja-literate travelers don't visit other camps without announcement.

Surprisingly, he recognized me from the previous year and fed me horror tales of the previous month's crowds.

"It was positively insane…beyond words. They were all just shitting in sand holes back of the point, and when the wind blew it exposed all this flapping paper…looked like filthy little Tibetan prayer flags. The coyotes got into it, had all this crap stuck to their coats. These idiots didn't even burn their paper.

"The worst were the characters who brought motorcycles and ATVs with them. They were totally free-ranging over the plants, tearing up the dunes, sloshing gas all over. It smelled like the Pomona Raceway with all the Castrol fumes.

"This was during the best swell I'd seen in four winters, so these squirrels think it's like that all the time. Federico has some powder and caps, and if it weren't for the fishermen we'd just blast the road."

After venting a bit more, he showed me the almanac he'd kept since his first year, and I noticed little notations regarding visiting surfers: "New 4Runner, green. Irvine plate frames. Left broken glass, firework litter, and crapped on the trail."

Lord help that crew if they return, and God save them if they show him any ill will. No less than six grim-faced, machete-wielding shark hunters will materialize in moments.

Here on the *frontera*, it's deeds, not words, and when you pull a fisherman's son out of a crippling fever, you gain true respect.

La malicia va más allá de la realidad.
Malice leaves reality behind.

They called themselves the Order of the Grip. All four owned trailers near Baja Malibu and considered it an indignity to surf with those who didn't reside there. While a visiting group of surfers was in the lineup, a member of the Order would casually walk to the interloper's car, take out a pair of vise grips, and tear the valve stem from one of the tires. October marked the Grippers' Ball, and the member with the most valve stems on his necklace was honored.

Resourceful to a fault, the Grippers devised several car-crippling devices, including "the flapper," a 16-penny nail driven through a small square of plywood, and "the sputnik," a Dixie cup filled with plaster of Paris, bristling with roofing nails. Either of these were placed in front of a car's tires. As the vehicle drove off, the flapper would snap obscenely as the air slowly drained, or, in the case of the sputnik, the tire would simply explode.

The Grippers erected signs ("No Surfers!"), kept drooling, teeth-gnashing dogs, and verbally sounded any visitors. The trailer park's maintenance man was deputized, given a custom badge, and awarded a six-pack for every surfer denied entrance.

The Order of the Grip eventually came to be known by face and name and made ineffective, but their run deserves a place in Norte lore.

Al buenos entendedores necesitan pocas palabras.
The truly knowledgeable need few words.

The four sponsored surfers in the East Cape lineup were eating the new swell alive: carving, tucking, and cross-stepping to the six-beats-per-second of a power-winding Canon.

All aged under 21, they were so absorbed in their surfing that they scarcely noticed the sand rail and Baja Bug convening on the beach at the top of the point. Didn't much matter to the pros: It looked as if the intruders would keep their distance.

In the shorebreak, a couple of *pescadores* were wrestling in a 60-pound roosterfish they'd caught on a handline buoy rig fashioned from a Fabuloso bleach bottle. They had a six-foot log standing by so they could gill-thread it and drag the beast to their shack.

The photographer thought the men up the point looked familiar, and he trained his lens on them as they paddled out, whereupon they proceeded to trade glassy, overhead waves. Thinking little more of it, the shooter got back to handling the assignment at hand.

Back in California, he was pleasantly surprised to discover 16 frames of expats Pat Curren and Reynolds Yater, surfing as if the years between 1964 and 1994 had been stripped away in some reverse-meridian time vacuum.

> *Sobre gustos? No hay libro.*
> **Concerning tastes? There is no guidebook.**

Janocleto's family had lived by the spring since the 1880s, and their home had served as a traveler's rest stop for just as long. His handsome wife was renowned by surfers for her *machaca*, corn tortillas, and rigid Nescafé. The fact that they were roughly 40 clicks off the road and thereby tied to the peso, not the dollar, made the 90-cent tab a reality even in the '80s. While Jano regaled guests with stories of his grandfather going head to head with marauding Paipai Indios, his cowpoke sons would chuckle at the surfers' strange attire.

Jano's boys lived full-time in the official getup of Baja ranchdom: soccer uniforms (for Saturday) and jeans, boots, cowboy hats, and pearl-buttoned shirts (for the rest of the week). It made it easy. Before a trip, we'd hit Sears and buy a couple pairs of Toughskins and two embroidered cowboy shirts as goodwill gifts.

In the late '80s, we went through a depressing period of root-bound torpor and were unable to make our winter run, but the following season we cheered as their house came into view. I had the bundle of clothes under my arm and shouted *"¿Que onda?"* as I came through their door. Mamacita welcomed me and in one breath explained that the men were in the shed, things had changed, Jano had inherited some money, et cetera.

When the sons came out into the light, I almost lost it. The eldest was sweating in a motorcycle jacket buttoned to the neck, a yellow skunk-stripe dyed into his hair, heaving Brooklyn attitude. The youngest had a thin chain connecting his nosering and earring, a Christian Death t-shirt, and Doc Marten knock-offs. Janocleto materialized a moment or two later, saving me, and pointed to the satellite dish in the trees.

The bundle of Sears clothes remains stashed in my trunk to this day, buried along with my narrow, dimwitted naiveté regarding the Baja's ability to resist the information age.

THE WAVES

Ai, que curvas, y yo sin frenos!
Ah, what curves…and me without brakes!

Like any ripe, 1,000-mile stretch of coastline, Baja offers a spouting horn of beachbreaks, reefs, rivermouths, and shorepounds, but it's the right points that lodge the barren finger firmly in our imaginations. Until you've experienced a wide sampling of her offerings, it is impossible to fathom the range, the sheer variety of perfection available. From top-heavy, yawning boulder points to teasing, talcum-bottomed, thin-lipped cracklers to every possible variation in between…it's all out there.

What is it to surf these points? Well, if forced to draw a mean, it might go something like this…

The headland is roughly door-knob shaped, and you take-off around the outside corner. This section is exposed to the wind, but that's good. The offshore shingles the face, and after you've drawn a turn and start to really trim it out, there's a very audible chattering under your board. You should already be pumping a bit here to make the bowl that lets you into the cove, as the shoulder's starting to bend toward you, and it's impossibly long. You've already covered 50 yards. The ledge rears up now, and what first looked like long odds now wants a little hand drag, maybe to the elbow, to time the tube. You're not yet clear of the rocks, but it's so clean you want to hang out in there. If you really concentrate you can see out the hole, over the oncoming shoulder, into the bay, and south toward headland after headland that are doing approximately the same thing. But enough daydreaming. The tube squeezes you out and into a silky cutback section. Just as you rebound, the water turns from slate blue to what the VW people once called seafoam green. You've entered the actual cove, and the wave now runs down a sand point for, oh, a quarter mile or so, and it's a righteous game of cat and mouse, of stalls, lip hits, and cutbacks. Oh, yes, at mid-tide there's another bowl ("Section 19"). What started out as just overhead has finally diminished to ankle-high and still perfectly shaped, so you prone in and walk back to the beak of the point, stopping first for a pull from the beer you've left in the one shaded tide pool. It's a timing thing, but you're at the takeoff zone after a 20-yard paddle. Four more of these and you're done for the morning.

> *El mejor torero es el de la barrera.*
> **The best matador is the one with nice front-row seats.**

The Baja experience isn't about hairball waves, though it has those. If you're into dense, fear-laden, triple-O-head bombs, there are better regions. If you prefer fiercely hollow situations where elkhorn and brain coral grate the bottom of your board with each turn, keep looking. Wave-wise, Baja's refined. Points, and lots of them. Cobble points, stone points, river, cliff, and sand points, wind-blown points and sheltered points.

The challenge is not so much "Can I surf this place?" but "Am I savvy, resourceful, and lucky enough to get it with all the elements in tune?"

WHAT IT TAKES

> *Aunque le jaula sea de oro, no deja de ser prisión.*
> **While the cage may be of gold, it is nothing but a prison.**

The salvation is this: Those with high-maintenance families, fat alimony bills, and long-hour careers—most of America, statistically—really don't stand a chance of scoring. That puts the odds in the favor of a) trust-funders and remittance chums, who generally fly in or hang out in Cabo, or b) down-and-outers, Humboldt vendors, and the self-employed who can drop tools at the hint of a swell.

Baja doesn't much care how many hours you've stared at the space maps. It doesn't abide by your 900 numbers. It sure as shit doesn't want any truck with your alt.surf.weather@aol.com log-ins. With all due respect to the freelance swell gurus, it's still a coin toss.

Chubascos buttonhook erratically, hit uncharted cold-water pockets, and camp on the rude side of offshore islands. Heinous fogs bloom, fostering onshores that blow like stink for weeks. Flash floods strip every grain of sand and deliver them to the Revillagigedos. Deep southern hemi's pull no-shows.

But. Don't forget the beachbreaks on the "wrong" side of the points. On their day, they can be hard offshore, steeple-peaked, and spitting like camels. All of this is a way of reinforcing the fact that you need time. *Tranquilo* is the order of any Baja venture. Try some side routes. Sit out storms. *Abren tus pinches ojos, mijos.*

> *El que temprano se moja tiempo tiene de secarse.*
> **He who gets drenched at dawn has the rest of the day to dry out.**

They parked close to the bluff's edge. Perhaps too close. All three fell asleep right where they sat, bone tired after the six-hour flog from San Diego. Sometime before dawn the first raindrops fell, waking the oldest. He'd camped this area before and knew what the rain meant.

"Get up! Right now! We gotta get outta here!"

Much grumbling and all were roused, and the van fired up.

"Man, last time I was here and it rained we were stuck for four days. This clay goes to grease. It'll be screwed less we get real lucky...come on!"

The wheels started spinning right from the get-go, finding only enough purchase to creep along at 5 mph, engine red-lining. By the time they reached the hill, it was getting ridiculous.

Gathering steam as best they could, they still went sideways halfway up, the tires throwing up huge plumes of red mud.

"Oh, man, we're done."

They all piled out and had a look. The old Dodge van free-slid another 10 feet, sending them scattering. By now it was dumping rain, and the gusting wind clocked west.

"We need traction."

Being a man of action, he scouted around and started tearing plants apart, stuffing them under the drive wheel. Nothing could have possibly looked more futile. The driver, still not yet fully awake, spied a trash heap up the hill. On inspection, it proved to be a midden of flattened Tecate cans, the detritus of some farmer's weird dirt ritual. He loaded his shirt and carted some back to the van.

"Will these help?"

"Yeah, you got it...we'll make a tin-can road!"

The three started a sort of bucket brigade, laying two strips of cans up the hill. The driver revved it up, threw it in gear, and punched it. As the van sank slowly into the earth it shot hundreds of cans out the back, buzzing like shrapnel. Again, everyone dove for cover. The front wheels were cantilevered off the ground, high-centered on a bump. Still the rain poured.

"Someone's gonna have to walk for help. I'll stay here with the ride...try to figure something out. You guys hit the road.

It's only about five miles to the *ejido*. See if anyone has a tractor."

The two of them started off, sinking to the knee with each step. The rain kept on coming. The sunrise was just a light glow through the clouds when they arrived, muttering like Tourette's sufferers, covered with mud. The lights were still off in all the dwellings, so they wandered the streets, unsure of how to proceed. Eventually, they came to a house with a large outbuilding, a green John Deere visible through the doors.

They walked through the gate and were set upon by the geese. A 30 pounder flapped up and took a small chunk out of one's cheek. The quicker one dove, screaming, right into a barbed-wire fence. The commotion woke the inhabitants, and the *patrón* came out with what looked to be a Civil War sword, slicing at the geese and cursing loudly.

After some pleading, the tractor was started and driven out of the compound. Half the *ejido* joined the procession, the John Deere leading, the surfers behind it, and 10 or 15 farmers following in a quest for entertainment. The one surfer held the hem of his t-shirt to his face to quell the bleeding goose bite.

An hour later the parade arrived back in town, the van chained to the tractor, and negotiations began in earnest. "One hundred dollars," the farmer said. "Twenty dollars," they said. "Seventy-five dollars," he said. "Forty dollars," they said. "Fifty and your peanut butter, those *Playboys*, and that bourbon," he said. "Deal," they said.

Within moments the farmer and his friends were staring bug-eyed at the brazen gringas in the magazine, tearing away just long enough to drive spoons into the jar of Superchunk.

The surfers thanked the farmer and piled in, resisting the urge to chuck it and head back north, pulling instead to the right, toward drier climes.

> *El que con coyotes anda aullar se sueña.*
> **If you run with the coyotes, you need to learn how to howl.**

Even before Kentucky mercenaries were hired to bounty hunt Comancheros, Mexico was a land imbued with blood, sand, and death. At times the old ghosts rear up on their hind legs and wail. Occasionally, it pays to help them along.

Not so long ago, a trio was suffering through a classic example of an old-fashioned skunking. No amount of fishing or reading could offer relief. As often happens in these situations, the two focused their efforts on the one. The one was a proper target, as he was older, and because he shoveled out perfect rain channels around his tent, and he dressed like Eddie Bauer on safari, and he never wiped his hands on his shirt, and he was undergoing a period of religion and would not drink liquor.

He stood on the rocks up on the lava point for hours, endlessly casting and reeling in heroic poses.

The two hiked up the beach to see what they could find. First they discovered a porpoise corpse, and they took the head with a camp hatchet and stuffed it in a sack. Next, they collected a sampling of sea lion and pelican skulls. These too they placed in the sack, and completed the hunt with the ribs of a coyote. Sweat pouring, they dragged the grim remains back to camp.

Still he casted, his rod tip whipping like D'artagnan's sword, oblivious to the goings-on near the truck. They constructed a crude rib-bone fence around his tent, topping the posts with skulls. Next, the head was unwrapped and placed on his inflatable pillow. They headed into the dunes to secure a surveillance point.

He broke down his fishing kit, hoisted his bucket, and walked back to camp. Without missing a beat, he circumnavigated the tent. With decorum and near British civility, he bowed to each skull.

They watched bewildered as he entered the tent, sat a while, and exited with no apparent emotion. He goose-stepped to the wooden box and grabbed the pint of tequila, draining the remaining 18 ounces in one solid pull. He turned on his heel, stared directly to their hiding place, and saluted smartly.

The circle completed and the scorners scorned, the swell, of course, began to rise.

DISCOVERY

Mar tranquilo hace mal marino.
Tranquil seas make poor sailors.

Consultation of old magazines won't help. Asking around will yield more false clues than solid information. Books in print offer no assistance. What remains is this: If you want it, go find it.

For me, the breakthrough came on my fourth trip to a particularly wave-laden region. We'd been worrying the coastal track for ages in an attempt to find a certain legendary half-point. We knew we were in the general vicinity—say, within 50 miles—and we'd picked a campsite at a wind-shadowed point to rest for the next day's exploration.

Already there were two older surfers from Pacific Beach. I came to realize that they were heavily credentialed Bajadores, so I smoothed my way in with a liter of Hornitos. I set the bottle down on their pine camp table and tried to ignore the words scrawled on the wood. It served as a log of their trips together and included wave size, duration, conditions, and crowd. The first entry was dated 1959. Paydirt.

I spent a long evening with them, carefully memorizing every applicable listing carved in the table.

Before I left, the older one pulled me aside. He'd seen my eyes light on the table. He told me that it was the most sacred object in his possession and noted that it represented 23 years of journeys. I told him that I'd never utter a word to anyone, and I've kept my promise ever since.

This is how priceless information is passed on. If you limit your crew to two, if you show basic camp preservation literacy, if you lay low and don't draw attention to yourself…you'll reap the education of those who came before.

My friend and I drove off the next morning, our heads swimming with our new-found direction. Six hours later we topped a bluff, hiking the last few hundred yards as the truck couldn't possibly survive the cholla cactus thicket. The point was shaped like a natural amphitheater with a left on one side, a right on the other, and a perfect sand peak in the center. We broke out in gooseflesh and found the trail in. The water was cool green, with the channels marked by deep blue. My partner ran back to the truck and erased our tread marks with a piece of brush.

We camped there for a week straight, cleaned the place up, and split.

Similar discoveries are still possible. Head down with the express intent of getting absolutely no surf, and you'll have a good time. Plan on breaking your vehicle. Know that you'll get buried in the *polvo* the minute you stray. And when you cross *la linea* on your way home, make a vow with your running mate to never spill the beans.

The bulk of the Mexican proverbs, or dichos, *that serve as story breaks in this piece are posted on the wall at Pancho Villa's Bar at K-29. Translation courtesy of Hector Nogales.*

It Must Have the Smoke

Interview: Javier Plascencia

From *The Surfer's Journal*, Volume 27, Number 6, 2018

•

San Miguel, the cobble-point rivermouth just north of Ensenada in Baja California Norte, is a source of origin for Mexican surfing. First regularly ridden in the 1960s by native pioneers Nacho Félix Cota and Carlos Hernandez, the dependable right offers a broad swell window and easy access. Trace the Guadalupe River from its outlet up a chaparral barranca, and you'll quickly find yourself in the Valle de Guadalupe. Here on the Ruta del Vino, the pebbled alluvia bears comparison to the flinty terroir of France's Rhône Valley. The climate scans Mediterranean, with the same dusty gray-greens and lavender colorations speckling the sun-cured landscape. This is the site of Tijuana restaurateur and surfer Javier Plascencia's most recent project, Finca Altozano.

In the decomposed granite parking lot of this vineyard "camp," Plascencia keeps a restored trailer for himself and his dog within earshot of the popular establishment's proceedings. An ancient, but well-kept, avocado-green Mercedes sedan is parked out front. Plascencia cuts a rugged, understated first impression. Work boots. Vintage Persol shades. Four-day growth. Fifty-one years old at the time of writing, he's soft spoken and thoughtful, choosing his responses in a measured way. Like the Nebbiolo and Tempranillo grapes surrounding the Finca, Plascencia comes from well-documented rootstock. Born to the trade, he scurried unabashedly around the various kitchens of his father, learning knife skills and the incalculable value of mise en place. He was a journeyman chef before he could drive a car.

His big break—one that he himself engineered—came in 2011 with the opening of Mision19, a restaurant that helped define a new international cuisine based on the peninsula's substantial bounty. "Baja Med" found instant purchase in food media, and the chef found himself unable to hide. The late Anthony Bourdain visited and filmed. Dana Goodyear profiled him with a 12,000-word doorstop in *The New Yorker*. Pulitzer-winner Jonathan Gold effused over his short rib in fig leaves. With such auspicious notices, the dedicated surfer had placed his dusty, generally lawless border metropolis, Tijuana, squarely in a constellation that includes Lyon, Shanghai, San Sebastián, Puebla, and Bologna—lodestars of gastronomy.

His raw supply chain was discovered during local surf trips. His flavor palette is familiar to any observant Baja wave rider. Maguey (agave) leaves. Rabbit. Yerba buena. Sea urchins. Bluefin tuna. Quail. He merged new-school technique with a Kumeyaay pantry, creating alchemy with mesquite smoke.

While now a household name in culinary circles, Plascencia is hardly doing victory laps. He shuttles between a demanding schedule of business and family operations up and down the peninsula. Surfing vents off the back pressure. Over a plate of charred octopus *tostaditas* and a local white wine that tasted like a fresh 10-peso coin dropped in a glass of lemon blossom water, he submitted to our brief grilling.

SH: How did you come to surfing?
JP: I was introduced to it in Carlsbad at 16. I went to the Army and Navy Academy. I got kicked out of school in Tijuana and, as punishment, my parents sent me there. And I'm very grateful to them because, I mean, I learned about surfing. My room was very close to the beach—walking distance. Every morn-

ing for reveille we had to march in our uniforms with rifles. But I had a great time and my roommate was a surfer. He got me into it.

SH: What was your impression of surfing growing up in Tijuana? Did you see surfers when you went to the beach?

JP: No, not much. When I was, like, 14, I used to take the bus with my friends to Rosarito Beach, and we would bring boogie boards. That was our thing. But I didn't know about surfing and I didn't meet any surfers until I came back from school. My friends that started boogie boarding with me became surfers as well.

SH: Any recollection of your first sled?

JP: It was a Gerry Lopez that the school had for everybody to use. My first personal board that I bought with my own money was from San Miguel Surfboards.

SH: When you came back to Tijuana from Carlsbad, I assume you continued to surf locally...

JP: I did, yeah, yeah, I did. My parents owned a house in Rosarito and that's where we started. We built a bar called Coco Loco. And I surfed a lot in Quinta del Mar, right in front of my house. Then, with my friends, I started going to K-38 a lot, and that's where I like really, really fell in love with, you know, the whole life and met the real locals that were there back in the '80s.

SH: I have a pet theory that Mexico might be the most naturally gifted country for surfing on Earth. From Todos to Salina Cruz, from Scorpion to Puerto Escondido to Pascuales. Pound for pound, it's worth considering. What is your impression of the national surf resource?

JP: I mean, I agree with you. I've surfed all over Baja. I've been to Oaxaca several times, down to Escondido. I've been to Michoacán. I travel a lot throughout the world and I always try to go surfing, but it's often crowded or flat or cold. Even though there are many more local surfers and tourists coming to surf now, you can usually find an empty wave [in Mexico]. And you still get that Baja vibe, which is very rural and Third World. It's just hard to get anywhere. You still feel like you've discovered something really amazing. It's something that when you just talk about it, it's very different. You have to live it.

SH: Where do you surf these days?

JP: Well now, I love K-38 because it's such a fun wave and it's perfect for my surfing. I don't surf big waves. I like Popotla. The left is very, very fun. Those two places, and El Morro. We have a villa at K-38, so it's very easy for us to go there. It's where we keep our equipment and where we do all of the friends-and-family things. Now our family comes, our kids come, and we have big gatherings and surf and do carne asada. When I went there as a kid—after they started building those condominiums—they would kick us out. They wouldn't allow us in. Eventually, we made friends with the guards. But when I saw those, I said, "Fuck, I wish I could buy a place so I can just surf here all my life." And now it's become true. We have a cam and we can watch it from the kitchen in the restaurant. So we know when it's good.

SH: Do you know anything about the surfing history of Baja, such as it is? Juan Hussong and Ricardo Dominguez and that first generation of locals?

JP: I know them and I talk to them. Jacinto, he still owns a surf shop in Rosarito. All those guys that were locals at that time when we were growing up, we looked up to them and they were like our idols. They were hardcore. There are several guys that I've seen lately that still surf.

SH: What do you think about the idea of Tijuana as a surf city, with Playas and the world-class beachbreak at Baja Malibu just minutes away?

JP: Definitely in Playas. I think it is the biggest surf community in Baja if you find all those kids that live there, because it's so close. A lot of kids walk or take their bike. I used to surf there a lot when I had my restaurant in Plaza Fiesta in Zona Río. I'd wake up early in the morning and go surf Playas and then come back to the restaurant. Some of my friends go there and surf in the afternoons when they get off work. I mean, we used to go surf Rosarito and come back fast and get back to work. Now, it's very hard because it's growing so much. It's very urbanized now. So there are a lot of people going and coming back after work.

SH: Sure, like any big city. But you're proof of it. A surfer could live in Tijuana and get all the benefits of that vibrancy and action and food and the art scene and maintain a surfing life too—at a quarter of the cost of San Diego.

JP: Totally. A lot of surfers love to come to Tijuana and have a good time. I mean, it's always been like that. I think surfers now are, you know, more cultural. They're not like the surfers that used to come and drink cheap beer. Now they smoke better weed and they drink better beers and they're into wine and they're into food, and it's just fun. I mean, when I'm in the lineup that's what I talk about with friends or with the people that recognize me or that go to my restaurants.

SH: What's a go-to after-surf meal for an internationally renowned chef? I mean, if you've had a two-session day and you're just ruined. What do you think of when you come home? What do you want to eat?

JP: I want to eat mostly seafood, like tostadas, ceviche, fish tacos. That's what I crave, and a really good beer or a wine. Sometimes pizza.

SH: Your family's pizza connection vibrates for me. When my great-grandparents came to San Diego in the 1940s, their go-to restaurant was Filippi's Cash & Carry on India Street. That's been our family joint ever since. And your dad, obviously, had a connection to that shop. That's kind of the beginning of the dynasty, right?

JP: Yeah, he learned to make pizza just sitting on the counter there in Little Italy. And he opened the first pizzeria in Tijuana back in 1968. So, it's going to be 50 years. But [the Tijuana version] is Giuseppe style, like New York style, and that flavor is very stuck in me. So when I get the munchies, that's where I go.

SH: Indigenous Baja foods like roasted agave tips and wild honey, chocolate clams, pitahaya, venison, things like that...does that maintain a presence in modern Baja cooking?

JP: Yeah, a lot. The chefs that are doing Baja-style cooking are taking the time to learn what ingredients people used to cook with and how they cooked. So we learned that all the Natives cooked with wood—live fire, because there was no gas. So they used mesquite or any wood that they could find. And they charred a lot of stuff. They cooked abalone and lobsters right on the fire. That's why when you taste Baja cuisine, there is always some type of smokiness. They have to be cooked on fire or charcoal, or it doesn't taste authentic for us. But, yeah, they cook with a lot of flour tortillas in the northern part of Baja, not a lot of corn. Lots of deer. Quail was big around this area. Rabbit too. They used to eat horse meat as well. All the *machacas* are very popular in the north of Baja California. So, they make *machaca* with lobster, and *machaca* with shrimp and fish. I remember when I was growing up, every Sunday my father took us to this place where he ate *caguama* (turtle) soup. That was a big thing for him on Sunday, I think because he'd be kind of hungover. I remember I couldn't handle it at the time. That smell was kind of very strong for me. But he took us, and I still remember how he enjoyed it. I learned to eat it and I enjoyed it when I was a little bit older, in my twenties. Now it's illegal, but I still remember that smell and that flavor. So we make "*caguama* soup" today, but it's made with manta ray and tuna. Another truly Baja ingredient would be *totuava*—those big, oily cuts of fish from San Felipe—but now we get that farmed. And also the abalones. It's something that's going away. You can still find it, but nowadays cooks are learning to work with farm-raised abalone. We support those companies because I think it's very important to preserve what we have still in the ocean and not to overfish it. But like my kids, they don't know what a big abalone tastes like or they've never seen it big, the way I saw it when I was a kid. Also lobsters. They're farm raised. It's still good, but it's not the same.

SH: How do you break up your time between your businesses in Tijuana and Todos Santos and here in the Valle?

JP: Well, when you're away, it's not always going to be the same as if you are here all the time taking care of stuff. I mean,

I just got here and I saw 10 things that I really was disappointed with. I just took my guys and said, "Come on, what's going on?" But I use phones, cameras. I run six restaurants that are under my name, but also my family runs 13 restaurants that I help out, you know, with events, menus, and that kind of stuff. Plus, I do seminars and talks and cooking demos—those kind of events. So it's tough. I'm in and out. I'm on airplanes a lot. What hurts most, what I don't like about this, is that it takes a lot of time away from my kids and also from surfing. But it's my passion. You have to have really good people. I mean any business, but especially in this hospitality business, you have to have a very, very good staff. They are part of the family. We take really good care of our managers and our chefs. We travel with them. They run the show. So I can go surfing.

SH: *What class of tequila do you favor?*
JP: I am more of a mezcal drinker. I prefer the ones from Durango.

Windows on Peru

Coca drip, beef heart, and leg-quaking lefts.

From *Surfer*, Volume 51, Number 11, 2010

•

Yesterday's surf spots are today's anachronisms. Our collective attention pushes ever forward. Makaha to Backdoor. Uluwatu to Greenbush. Stoner's to Barra. In some cases, entire countries find themselves in the elephant's graveyard. In the '50s and '60s, Peru was the locus of South American surfing. Today, our gaze has shifted across the border to Chile. Does that mean Peruvian waves have fallen out of fashion? Peru herself? Both fair questions. Cream, for the most part, rises. Go-to spots of lore have become mere base camps as exploration turns up mind-blowing discoveries. But in an age where a $5,000 boat trip leads to a crowded lineup, an old warhorse can still trot the course with style.

Like anywhere, Peru is branded with accepted notions. You've heard them, and they're not all good. Lefts only. Cold water. Cocaine whiteouts. Dodgy street food. Hairball crime. Overrated, dribbling points. Most stereotypes are built on a kernel of truth, and Peru is no exception. But nothing is so liberating as seeing them shattered in the face of stoking surprise.

That alone is hard to do in Peru. This isn't Bali. You don't fly in, organize a taxi, and light out for your hotel. For starters, odds are fair that your airport cabbie will "stop for a pack of smokes," where knife-wielding accomplices will climb in and drive you straight to an ATM. It's called "express kidnapping." Likewise, it's ill-advised to drive unaccompanied to the northern points on the Pan-Am Highway. There is zero police presence and some vestiges of anti-gringo sentiment. Here, that not only means anti-foreigner but anti-non-Indigenous. Devastating poverty leads not only to crimes of opportunity, but jackings of a decidedly violent stripe. Unlike some other Latin American countries, like Mexico, crime isn't just clique on clique. White boys get jumped.

It doesn't matter how roots level and soul daddy you roll. You have things, and the *rateros* want to take them. This isn't blogosphere fear-mongering. Once in-country, you'll hear all the first-person vignettes you can stomach.

There are compelling reasons for having "a friend in Peru." Local homies make it their business to lead you to empty surf, clean food, and paranoia-free travel. That doesn't mean it will be pre-packed and sanitized. To the contrary, guides will lead you to deeper interaction, clipping you into an outrageous level of local knowledge.

I dropped down solo last May, asking my Peruvian friends to surprise me, to show me *their* Peru. They obliged, and we enjoyed some fine waves. Beyond that, they offered windows into the country I never would have found on my own.

THE SOFÍA FACTOR

Peruvians cluck about her in protective tones. She has an Eastern Euro catwalk name courtesy of her Croatian heritage. She is the first South American surfer to win a world title. She has achieved something close to ubiquity in her land. Which is saying something.

Only a few of her countrymen have ever garnered kitchen-table recognition and global renown. Photographer Mario Testino, chef Gastón Acurio, and novelist Mario Vargas Llosa come to mind. But as a sporting figure, Ms. Mulánovich speaks to an even more populist base.

When a Peruvian finds that you've come to their country for waves, Sofía Mulánovich's name is floated like a balloon of potential connectivity. Taxi hacks, money changers, socialites, sushi chefs—all consider Sofía and surfing inseparable. A visiting surfer's level of enthusiasm for her skill and accomplishment connotes respect for the country at large.

This is particularly true in the cluster of surf towns south of Lima. Punta Hermosa and San Bartolo are the home of the Mulánovich clan, an extended family with decades of surfing behind them. Infested with reef waves, the area serves up everything from cracking little lefts to the elevator drops of Pico Alto.

You can watch the chocolate-chip-shaped waves of Pico fold over through the windshield wipers. It's not rain; just the wet, perennial fog the locals call *la gana*. A Californian feels comfortable here in the year-round June gloom. Pico is double overhead-plus, a touch ruffled, and no one out. Indeed, even with five spots seen breaking from this vantage, that's the theme: emptiness. Back home, there would be 30 surfers clotted in each takeoff zone. Midweek on the outskirts of Lima, it seems no one can be bothered.

It tells you much about how La Gringa—a local term of endearment for the fair-haired Sofía—was able to hone her program. She still lives up the bluff, with a buffet of options at her feet. Hell, she's up the street now, checking it from her window.

BONE-SCAPE

Alberto is strapped. Running the highway between Trujillo and Paiján, he assures us that he needs to be. Barring a full frontal with AKs, his throated and stippled Colt .45 should come over the top if an impromptu roadblock materializes. He's been prepaid and vetted and is a trusted source of transport for visiting surfers.

We cross the Río Chicama. Cutting through giant sugar plantations, its Andean runoff looks too meager to support the vast tracts of cane. Turning left of the Pan-Am at the cockfighting arena, we bounce down the road until we come to a sign. Punta Malabrigo: *La ola mas larga del mundo.* The town of Chicama is windswept, dirty, and bedraggled. An Ennio Morricone soundtrack waiting to happen. Overfishing led to the closure of the town's sole revenue stream, and fishmeal plant stands shuttered. Nearly a hundred tuna seiners are anchored into the teeth of the wind, pulling at their rusting chains. The surrounding plains and hills are bare earth. The flora…there is no flora.

Suddenly we're through the gates of the resort. From the outside, it's vaguely Fort Apache, with 8-foot walls and electrified fencing. Inside, it's like an expensive hit of oxygen. Charlotte Gainsbourg spills from hidden speakers. The architecturally splendid structure is oriented to keep the wind out and the point waves front and center. From the freighter bridge-like lounge, a pair of tanned Lienerias are evident poolside, sucking on pisco sours. The surf below is small and crisp in the offshores. It's only shoulder-high, but taut, high-pocketed little walls strip off down the bay. In the vanishing point distance they are small and well-turned. As they begin to feel the bar, they swell, doubling in size, gaining muscle curvature and magnetic force. By the time they reach the inside racetrack section of El Hombre, they're suddenly round in all the right ways.

The cape is two miles long. There's no one out, so I feel 14 percent less ridiculous crawling over the gunwale of the Zodiac for the run out to the tip. Somebody drops the quip of the day:

"It's like heli-skiing the bunny slope." The Chicama native on the tiller isn't complaining. This is the first time he's ever had a paycheck. We tumble over the side and paddle to the lineup. Even on a 2-foot day the current is ripping. It takes a half-dozen waves to make it back to the town. Long enough for a matchbox-size wad of coca leaf and baking soda to disintegrate between cheek and gum.

Leaving the resort, the contrast is gut wrenching. We walk into town with a payload of clothing my guides have collected for their village friends. The streets are empty, and most storefronts are boarded up. We pass by a pharmacy, its name on a banner over the door: "*Mi Mama no me Quiere.*" My mommy doesn't want me.

I'm introduced to some local connections. Pajarete is the heavy. His English nickname is "Johnny B. Good." He's built like a street-trained trachea breaker and spent five years in a São Paulo prison. He holds things down on the point, gives surf lessons to the odd Euro backpacker, and operates a small hostel. In a town with a sketchy reputation, some solo travelers have found a sort of symbiosis by staying with Pajarete. He knows the territory here and walks the beat daily. Next door you'll find Pajarete's friend, Zorro, a native Chicameño who runs a surf-photography business. If a pebble rolls down the hill, these two know about it. It is said that they are masters of procurement.

Back at the resort, the watchman opens the portal. Before he got the job he was a *huaquero*—a grave robber. Guided by night shadows and the hallucinogenic effects of San Pedro Cactus, he wandered the plains looking for telltale hillocks. Sometimes he found pottery or precious metal, other times unmarketable skeletons. Not all of the bones were ancient. The entire Peruvian coastline is an archeological dig waiting to happen. Kick your boot into the sand behind the fishmeal plant and you turn up a skull.

PRE-PIZARRO

Pachacámac is a sort of coastal Machu Picchu constructed entirely of adobe. It's just south of Lima, moments from the reefs of Hermosa. Its scope takes in square miles, crowned by a lofty temple with a clear view of the dumping waves of the Lurin Rivermouth and Isla Ballena just offshore. We think of the Inca as a purely mountain people, but their empire spanned from Ecuador to Argentina. Pachacámac was an important administrative center, taking its sustenance from agriculture on the alluvial flats and seafood from the Pacific. Foot runners would relay fresh lobster to priests in the high Andes. The ocean was primary and was fished from the backs of *caballitos de totora*, the small reed surf craft of the ancients. Ocean studies were paramount, from here in the south to Chan Chan in the north.

The most beautiful women in the land were brought here to live in communal luxury, learning the crafts of the culture. In times of crisis, several of them would be culled from the group and marched to the top of the temple.

In the adobe city, a typical "time of crisis" was the El Niño. Rain and mud make poor stablemates, and entire towns melted away. The Inca charted the Humboldt Current on frescoes in an attempt to forecast the phenomenon. When all efforts failed and the storms materialized, the priests assembled on their sandstone thrones and lives were sacrificed.

Every river valley on this coast has an ancient city on its banks, a shared story.

CERRO AZUL

We drive two hours south of Lima to the town of Cerro Azul. The place was Gypsy Jet Set in the '60s, but today the attention has turned 1,000 miles north to the gob-smacking barrels of Cabo Blanco and the comparably chic town of Pacasmayo. The little bay reads like a left-breaking blend of Leo Carrillo and Malibu: a scallop of clean sand, a pier, and a rock outcropping at the takeoff.

We hit it at dawn the next morning. Glassy, overhead, and stunningly empty. Standing thigh-deep in the waiting room behind the rock, a pair of sleek shapes dart by. "¿Hay nutria?" I ask. Peruvian sea otters. Outside, a set spokes through. Dolphin explode from the wave faces, doing go-behinds all the way to the pier. They're the only thing keeping the wave resource from going totally unexploited.

Surveying the beach, I catch a pair of surfers eyeballing us. In a nod to old-school traveler's style, they defer to the peak breaking on the north side of the pier. The beachside restaurants are starting to stir. I can't imagine how they keep it rolling if we're the only trade.

Cerro has a civilized, if overcast, feel. At dinner one evening, I picture myself decades down the tracks, living as a pensioner here, surfing point waves into my dotage and living carefully on social security checks and orphaned paperbacks. Maybe a "Stay thirsty, my friends" sort of beachfront dishabille, or Graham Greene in Katins. On cue, a grizzled American surfer walks by our table, not sparing the time to say good evening. Maybe he just has a good book waiting. That new Christopher Hitchens or something.

The Peace

A visit to Isla Cerralvo.

From *The Bight*, Volume 2, Number 2, 2018

•

We're forced to be social. We grit our teeth and answer phones, emails, texts, coworkers, family, friends, and, if we're lucky, a few worthy enemies. Many of these exchanges are pleasant. Others procedural. A few are four-chaptered root canals. Sociologists assure us that constant interaction is healthy, that it instills a sense of something called "community." Balls.

Too much social interaction will kill you faster than a hangman's punchline.

It's easy to find yourself eating your stress. Smoking it. Drinking it. Becoming it. I'm using this space to tell you this: Don't wait until you're teats-up in some business park as EMTs tuna-spike you with a seven-gauge syringe to do something about it. ("Is it too late to start jogging?" asks the old saw.)

There are signs, and it does not profit you to ignore them. Rapid breathing. Retinal floaters. Unintentional sneers. Sexual disinterest. Behavior more *Rattus norvegicus* than *Homo sapien*. It can become chronic. You'll know when your traditional exhaust vents no longer bring relief. When you find yourself 50 miles offshore glassing for bird and the appearance of a few unanticipated boats raises your hackles. You need to practice self-rescue. And while I don't know *the* answer, I know *an* answer.

I was showing several of the markers listed above this spring. My lizard brain went to work. I needed to be rounding a chain of austere headlands in an unmarked panga, speaking sparse jailhouse Spanish with some *lanchero*. Over my 50-some years, I've found that I have more in common with the values of the average coastal Baja dweller than I do with someone from, say, Utah or Michigan. For that reason, I consider myself as much Californio as American. Despite arbitrary lines drawn on a map, shared interests unite the coastal citizenry of Mexico and the Bight. In my world, a solid voting block would run from Point Conception—the Chumash Western Gate—south to the Tip, around the horn, and up to Isla Montague at the mouth of what now passes for the Río Colorado. Call it the Mossback Republic. Currently accepting flag designs.

Four days of immersion would be about right. A mere rescue dose, but enough to drop the blood pressure a few points.

Baja destinations are never selected lightly. I've refused to establish an ownership beachhead because every spot has its bluebird season. You need to pivot. December on a Pacific *punta* lacking even a mapped name. October at Animas. June near La Ribera. September below El Rosario. Every bush vet has his own calendar and waypoints.

It was April when I had to take myself out of circulation. Tough month, April. From experience, that meant somewhere between San Jose del Cabo and Loreto. A hit-or-miss time for fishing, but always lightly attended and with brilliant weather, smack in the sweet spot between the howling nortes and the hotbox of summer. Something in my George Costanza wallet of a Baja library had me thinking of La Paz. I have scored in the past by revisiting places that have fallen out of media favor. The capital city, once a flashpoint for the fly-in set, has long been seen as played out, having lost tonnage of market share to its garish neighbor to the south. But I didn't want tournament-*landia*. I had little need for anything even remotely "Wabo." I don't require my marlin to giggle. A squat bottle of Bohemia would do.

Beyond that, I had run the coordinates. I reckoned that the perfect place to divorce myself from all things digital had a name: Punta Viejo, a sandy knob on the southern lee of Isla Cerralvo.

Legend says that this was the traditional burial spot for *los vagabundos del mar*, the sea tramps from Sonora. Whether or not that story holds water is beside the point. As viewed from satellite imaging, Viejo is a charismatic bulb of fat-grained white sand far enough off the mainland to lend it a touch of the forbidden. It also looks like some sort of roosterfish Valhalla, with far less pressure than you'd find on the peninsula proper. While not a fresh discovery—the island has been relentlessly fished since at least the '60s—the early season promised some open water.

The Mexican government recently renamed Cerralvo "Jacques Cousteau Island," to the derisive jeers of the locals. "Cerralvo" is not only poetry to the ear, it honors the memory of the Marquess of Cerralvo, the one-time viceroy of New Spain who funded its discovery by Capitán Ortega in 1632. With no disrespect meant to Cousteau, I join the Paceños in lofting a middle finger to the southeast at the municipal halls of Mexico City.

But back to this crisis of a fishing trip. Panic-hole selected, it was a simple matter to book a national flight out of Tijuana. The new cross-border pedestrian bridge at Otay is a game changer, offering friction-free access to the right-sized, modern, and friendly Rodríguez International. I was tail-drifting into La Paz before the morning caffeine had worn off.

A masthead colleague had introduced me to Jonathan Roldan, a broadly experienced outdoor writer and proprietor of Tailhunter International Sportfishing. Roldan long ago made it his quest to become a total authority on everything La Paz, with a laser focus on the fishing resource. Together with wife and business partner, Jill, Roldan oversees a small empire comprising a bar and restaurant, two panga fleets, and relationships with every hotel of standing. They took a personal interest in getting me away from the crush and onto some fish. Roldan's weekly reports from the area are often saluted for their honesty and lack of hype. Beyond that, his deep local knowledge shortcuts you to the heart of the local experience, as far from the braying Okies as you like.

The Spanish language has a beautiful verb meaning, specifically, to rise early: *madrugar*. The morning of my first full day, I found myself on the shoreline at Bahía de los Muertos in *la madrugada*. The southeastern lobe of Baja Sur is the only place I've ever seen a green-flash sunrise. It was the sort of thing that would have had Bronze Age primitives chittering and rolling their eyes and conjuring the supernatural. Knowing that it was the interplay of atmospherics and orbital mechanics did nothing to dilute its sacred magic.

Muertos failed to spit up a repeat performance of the flash, but it was a stunning morning nonetheless. Within minutes, we were fanging across the channel to Cerralvo. Pancho, my *panguero* from the fishing village of Agua Amarga, didn't bat an eye when I went over the rail at Viejo. Within a hundred steps, I was in the sixteenth century, crunching up the arroyo to make some photos of the point. Pancho did slow circles off the head of the sandbar, happily taking in the morning. Having counted coup on another *isla* in the Mossback Republic, it was time to get to work.

We fished, we caught, and have you ever seen a grip-and-grin photo of a guy cradling a roosterfish? Me too. About a million of them. Let's kill that cliché with words: It was as flamboyant as they all are, acrobatic, pissed, and just as strong when it finned away as it was when it hammered a slow-trolled *sabalo*. And, strangely, it was the *sabalo* that proved the more compelling catch.

As we drifted off of Punta Viejo, I had watched as Pancho twirled a piece of 50 over his head, lasso style. Swinging from the end was a bare treble hook cannibalized from a broken jig, augmented with a 1/2-ounce sliding egg sinker. He'd let it sink out a couple of feet before reefing it through the water. The *sabalo*—or ladyfish—would slam it on the pause. The ensuing show was like roosterfishing in miniature. The baitfish, big as a trophy rainbow trout, launched into the air, bucking and snapping and usually coming unbuttoned. About every fourth try one would stick and end up in the boat. It was clearly a good time. Pancho tried to hide that fact, but I'd have none of it. I went to school on him and was soon able to fling the near weightless rig 15 feet, rip it through the shallows, keeping everything taut enough to haul them in.

In a world where cow tuna boil within sight of Oceanside, ladyfishing is a difficult thing to defend, in these or any other pages. I found it perfectly antisocial. No beeps, whistles, or rings. Sight fishing with a simple handline. Feeling every twitch, hard against a deserted island of rock and sand, no human presence. Just me, a *panguero* who laughs while he works and has invented ribald lyrics to accompany current US pop tunes, and some cold *machaca* burritos and beers in the cooler.

I'm back now. Writing on my phone, for Chrissake. The carry-over effect from the trip has me breathing as calm and measured as a NATO sniper. But this phone is toggled to mute, and I'm white-knuckling these next few weeks until I drop back down south.

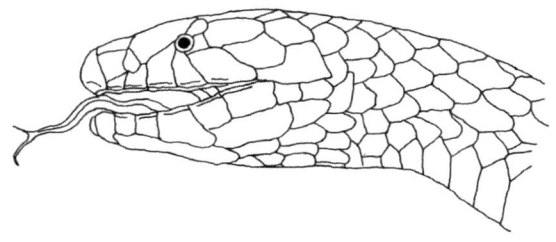

Night and the Iguana

If you have designs on surfing—or escaping from—a prison island, you're going to have to pay.

From *The Surfer's Journal*, Volume 30, Number 2, 2021

The occasional tourist wanders up from Mismaloya Beach below, but, for the most part, it is a silent and deserted place, its rough edges thankfully softened by the ever encroaching jungle. No one—other than an old man who passes there on an occasional trip between Las Caletas and Vallarta—seems to give a damn what happens to the place. He would like to see it torn down and given back to the iguanas. The old man is me of course.
—John Huston, *An Open Book*

Alcatraz, Devil's, Rikers, Robben. Prison islands imply dread with a floral note of the picaresque. Being forcibly marooned implies finality. Once moated in, a different sort of wall presents—one that can't be chipped away or tunneled under.

Like all island penitentiaries, Tres Marías, northwest of Puerto Vallarta, was notorious. The coastal mountains of the Mexican states of Nayarit and Jalisco lie 100 kilometers away, visible under the right conditions. On a clear day, the inmates could see the mainland. On summer nights, lightning illuminates the continental peaks from Tepic to somewhere above Mismaloya. These chimeric glimpses would have reminded one of home. Family. Girlfriends. Poor choices. Throwing in with the "wrong" party. Regret. Standing on the beach, the reality would come fast and hard. Hemmed in by heavy water. A channel too broad to be worthy of the name. The math of it would die in the mouth before the sum could be uttered.

Most of the incarcerated were inland people, not watermen. Escape would be foolhardy, even suicidal. Capture and punishment, or death by weather, sea creatures, or thirst. Only the most desperate or deranged would consider fleeing. Of the tens of thousands who lived and died there over a 110-year span, fewer than 90 made it past the shorebreak. Some were recaptured, others drifted for weeks before they were rescued, many were never found. Fifty or so, aided by complicit prison officials, bought the equivalent of high-priced charter boat rides.

Today, the prison is closed. The current president of Mexico, Andrés Manuel López Obrador, ordered it shuttered in 2019, and its fate sits in a sort of limbo. The prisoners are gone, the grounds lonely but for the sort of institutional echo that vibrates through places where tragedy was commonplace. Not that you can visit. The islands are off-limits, as they have been since 1905, when the prison was founded. For over a century, navy patrol boats and fast-attack gunships kept prisoners in and interlopers out. They actively patrol there still.

Why would people come? For money, mostly, but also for sport. The chain's biodiversity is well documented. As mainland fishermen deal with overextended resources, the islands' wealth of pelagics—tuna, dorado, and wahoo—and inshore species—chiefly pargo and seemingly endless fields of succulent conch—beckon like jewels.

Surfers, of course, are occasionally attracted to the islands. Phil Edwards, perhaps our culture's most enduring style icon, sailed past the chain in the mid-'60s on a wing-on-wing run from Cabo San Lucas to Puerto Vallarta. There was surf during his visit, and his crew carved what must have been first tracks. Sitting on his Capistrano Beach porch one afternoon in 1994, he answered a young *Longboard Quarterly* editor's hackneyed question of "What has surfing meant to you?" without a moment's hesitation: "Oh, it's the adventure." Surfing off the shore of a Mexican prison island (along with a lifetime of self-propelled coastal gunkholing) explains Edwards in a way that no almanac-style list of movie clips, surfboard models, and reader-poll victories ever can.

The period between Edwards' visit and the turn of the century is hard to document, but easy to dead reckon. Southbound cruisers sail past in November, and a handful of those vessels have boards lashed to the lifelines. Local surfing fishermen from the coastal villages of San Pancho, Sayulita, and La Cruz have ridden the main break sporadically. If the coast looks clear, they'll run the risk of sliding a few.

If a patrol boat catches you, you'll likely find yourself boarded, arrested, and towed to the island's naval dock for booking. It's not cheap and it's not pleasant and it happens every year. This isn't sneaking into the Ranch, and the result won't be a hand slap. It's a naval trespass violation in a Mexican district that made its bones sealing in some of the country's most dangerous felons: kidnappers, state enemies, transnational organized-crime gangsters. They're used to legitimate badasses. Callow newbs might quickly wish they had opted for that Instagram van life once they find their wrists slipped into a pair of *esposas*.

I was aware of all this before my first trip to the Marías, in 2015. I'd been invited down for a short week of gathering sashimi. Apparently, all papers were in order. The waters surrounding the islands are justifiably famous for cow-class fish: 200-plus-pound yellowfin tuna. Flying home with a freezer-stuffing load of A5 *maguro* sounded appealing. It was winter, so any thoughts of surfing there were off the table. Eleven of us motored out of Nuevo Vallarta on the *Maximus*, captained by Keith Denette. A pioneer of sorts, he was among the first Californian sportboat skippers to focus on the Marías fishery. Before that, it was the province of skilled expat sportfishermen and a handful of lights-out Mexican masters.

Denette, something of a maverick, was at first begrudgingly accepted by the locals. His near-immediate success and brash, limit-pushing style soon had some area captains aligning against him. The fact of the matter was that everyone was dancing on the edge, Mexicanos and visitors alike. Trophy tuna fishing remains a lucrative proposition, and life in the offshore Far West requires a gunslinger's swagger. Denette has some of that.

(Four years ago, Denette lost the *Maximus* on a repositioning run. In the cold current a hundred miles off Guerrero Negro, the boat's wooden hull delammed. Denette and two crew members crawled into the life raft at dusk and watched as the boat slipped under the waves. They had managed to radio a *Socorro!* (SOS) before going overboard. Miraculously, a passing barge—towing the Space Shuttle fuel tank, of all things—heard the signal and rescued them.)

Fishing offshore in the moonlight, the islands' buffer zone scans surreal. Pods of small, coffee-colored dolphins surround the boat, feeding on squid attracted to the deck lights. The mollusks are the size and shape of black, fat-handled baseball bats. Below them, refrigerator-size yellowfin hit glow jigs. One fights these ludicrous creatures drop-knee style with cannonball-heavy, two-speed reels resting on the rail. When a gaffed fish hits the deck, the thud shakes the hull clear to the bow. It's not dainty, and Norman Maclean failed to rhapsodize. The art of it lies in the interstice between getting bit and sliding the fish into the hold for an ice nap. That's when only bad things can happen—saw-offs, knot failures, line breaks, angler error, and the like. There's focus, technique, and muscle involved—if not finesse.

Many surfers are attracted to this game, local Mexicans chief among them. Diego Cadena, Dylan Southworth, and Juan "Pana" Muñoz all stab out to the zone for fishing and freediving. If the coast is clear, they dart inside to ride waves at a place Southworth jokingly calls "Disneyland."

"Oh, it's a mission," says Southworth. "The fuel expense, being in an open skiff trying to sleep. It's a long and dangerous run. You have to have your stuff together. It's not something we do all the time, but we love it any time we can make it happen."

Southworth and Cadena have fished and surfed the islands in a variety of ways: long and sketchy dark-to-dark runs, overnights on a rain-soaked panga, even camping in the thorn jungle. Employing surfing's long-standing Artful Dodger ethos, they've avoided arrest. Trading beer and tackle to local commercial panga fishermen, they clip into a stream of underground intel: "The patrol boat is waiting on a fuel separator and inoperable." "The *Marinas* (navy) are everywhere." "*Las pinches chotas consiguio a nuestros compas, incluso robando motor.*" ("The cops got our friends, and even took their outboard.")

This cat-and-mouse game means the waves are lightly surfed, even after a full-scale surf-media assault: *Surfing* magazine's 2009 Google Earth Challenge, the kind of exposure that led to Skeleton Bay's obscene overcrowding.

The Challenge—a combination print/online publicity stunt—involved *Surfing* challenging their readers to find "undiscovered" waves via satellite photos. The 2009 edition landed off the coast of Nayarit courtesy of Steven Page, the 12-year-old winner of the fourth GEC. He found one of the island's waves using Google Earth's flight-simulator function. *Surfing* arranged for young Page to join staffer Travis Ferré, photographer DJ

Struntz, pros Greg Long, Sam Hammer, and Ricky Whitlock, and local guide (and Mexican national champion) Cadena. The crew journeyed to the island, leveraging Cadena's knowledge of naval patrol patterns, and set up camp in the jungle for five days. Much of the piece was devoted to the hunting of a local black iguana. The islands crawl with them, and plumper examples are bush-tucker delicacies.

Shockingly, the group scored an unduplicatable confluence of swell and conditions. The swell direction and glass factor were such that the only hitch was the takeoff boil—a welcome complication on an otherwise too-perfect wave.

Ferré, the magazine piece's author, delivered an informed and entertaining documentation of the trip, matched by Struntz's beguiling photographs. Despite the obvious—searchable on Google Earth during a "swell day" satellite pass, Pacific dry-tropical Mexico, landmarks in evidence—the magazine opted against outright naming the place. Alas, from the day it saw print, a thousand fingers clutched a thousand mice. Any reasonably skilled, geography-minded surfer found the wave in the time it took for a bong rip to come on.

Astute students of surfing know what happened next… right? Wrong.

Had the Marías been at risk from truck-driving hominids from SoCal or Cape Town or Brisbane, it would have been overrun immediately by surf schools, yoga touts, bliss ninnies, and real estate slingers. But it wasn't, and still isn't, at risk. Distance, expense, and the navy see to that.

Since the wave's international debut, it has peeled off more or less by its lonesome, a handful of locals with boats playing risk versus reward during optimal swells. Maybe the odd sailboat cruiser, oblivious to consequence. Good waves are precious few. Nothing in winter. August is too late. Prime time is often scotched by side-off wind. Over the last decade, surfers made curious by the islands' wealth usually have opted for lower-hanging fruit. The consensus is that it's not worth it. When local charter skippers with a lifetime of connections find themselves locked up in a federal holding cell for trespassing, that doesn't inspire confidence in the offices of the surf-trip packagers.

Josh Temple knows this all too well. A Canadian charter captain and surfer, he plied his trade until about 2016, when he left Mexico—probably for good. Where controversy is concerned, he was pretty much unequaled in the Marías zone and in the international sportfishing community. Flamboyant and loquacious, Temple's online fishing reports were illustrated with record catches, tournament wins, and the occasional topless model. If one was looking to sell a charter to some snowbound insurance salesman in Tulsa hoping to recapture his libertine glory days, the approach was gold. Low-key it wasn't.

While Temple and his millionaire partners failed to permanently solve the Islas Marías access issue, they did temporarily crack the code. In a 360tuna.com post dated March 22, 2011, Temple shared his perspective:

"We finally started to realize that if we continued to push the limits someone was going to get seriously screwed. We were hearing stories of people actually going to jail, and having their boats taken.... We found out that there was a way to get permission to fish within the restricted zone. Supposedly if you knew the right guy in Mexico City, or Guadalajara, or Tepic, you could get weeklong permits to fish out there. So we started digging. Eventually, after a lot of time and effort and most importantly BRIBE MONEY

$$$ we connected with a guy who knew a guy, etc. And POOF! We had permits to go. So what do you do with that kind of paperwork? YOU GO! Our first trip on these permits was nerve wracking. We went all the way out to Isla Madre on a brand new custom yacht worth $3 million and winged it. Anyone who knows the details of THAT story can assure you that we were scared shitless and literally flying by the seat of our pants. But do you know what???? THE PERMITS WORKED!! And we had a great dinner at the prison/Naval base on our boat with the commandante [sic] and drank beers with the boys long into the night.

"Subsequently, power of control over the islands has also recently changed hands. Formerly controlled by the Navy in San Blas, the islands and the prison are now under SSP control. For those that don't know, the SSP is Mexico's version of the FBI, Secret Service, and CIA all rolled into one. You do not want to mess with these guys.

"In the old days you could outrun the patrol boat, no problem. We all did it. Then they got a go-fast patrol boat that you couldn't outrun…then we started to get caught with regularity, warnings became stern and severe. Then we found some permits. Things got much better for years. Then the chit [sic] hit the fan all at once. Authority and the seriousness of the cartel situation took precedence over a few boats wanting to catch tuna. The SSP started cracking down and dozens of people were made examples of…Now who do we have to bribe at the SSP to get access again? Somebody get me THAT guys [sic] name and number."

Temple has moved his base of operations back to Canada, but permits have indeed become the coin of the realm. At issue is *which* permit. Agencies, terms, and conditions are notoriously fluid. One vessel, the *Maria Cleofus* (née the *Royal Pelagic*), devised a way to come over the top. Learning that Mexican islands in general and the Marías in specific were protected as biosphere reserves, the owners of the *Pelagic* formed a California-based nonprofit and hustled up a research permit. The 128-foot ex-Alaskan crabber—now refitted as a luxury surf-expedition yacht—enjoyed favored-nation status. Hosting scientists and researchers in the lap of shipborne extravagance—"shag carpet, mood lighting, plush surround-sound theater, 6-burner Wolf Range, Greenough skiffs"—the vessel was most often found "on the hook" outside the surf spot. It is unlikely that anyone has surfed more waves at the Marías than the *Pelagic*'s lucky guests and crew. The combination of a federal permit and (until 2019) prison-island security represented a golden ticket.

I visited the Marías again in the winter of 2016, and a third time in 2018 on Denette's *Constitution*, the insurance replacement for the lost-at-sea *Maximus*. One night remains lodged in my notes. We were anchored in a cove near the surf spot, the sky above a lesson in Greek astronomy. Denette related that the cove was rarely visited.

"Well," he said, "it's too tucked in and too shallow for most. I have every rock marked, and nobody would think to look for you here. We're kind of hidden in plain sight."

Near midnight in the cove, fishing with light tackle for clouds of pompano, something caught my eye. An escapee. Holding fast to a raft of flotsam, the iguana drifted off into the dark. No marine creature, it was anyone's guess how this woebegone refugee had become detached from his home. Yet there he sailed, off to God knows where.

In the summer of 2020, I jumped on a Vallarta-based boat with a group of friends, including Southworth. Muñoz, a ripping local boxer in his forties, runs a booking agency called Saltmen. He served as our *ayudante* (deckhand) as well as "second ticket" (backup captain). I was hungry to see how the prison closure had changed the landscape.

We were assured we had a permit, and, with Muñoz and Southworth's local knowledge, we felt confident in our ability to absorb any bracing by the patrol boats. The ace in the hole was mounted on the roof of the flying bridge, quietly spinning away. Radar has always been a coveted component of the Marías surf experience. One can sit on the hook, alert for any suspicious blips on the screen. In the event of a fast-moving mark, you have, at bare minimum, time to get your documents at the ready, and in some cases can take the opportunity to weigh anchor, fire up the Caterpillars, and head for safe water. We ended up needing none of that. On this trip, our enemy was the wind.

Waiting for the trades, we worked through a compass clock of breeze, catching seconds of pleasure between the rough grain of sideshore chop. Even the crew was put off their feed by the wind. Albino, our taciturn Sinaloan mate, fiddled with the gold chain that draped around his neck and under one arm, *bandolero* style. The captain saw me studying him.

"He's getting ready to go ashore," he said. "To practice his religion."

We watched as Albino motored alone in the inflatable, around the break and toward the beach. An hour later he was still on the sand, marching a ritual pattern and pointing a stick at some prescribed directions. It was oddly solemn. Whether conjuring or giving thanks, we had no idea. It felt rude to ask. He had been on the island hundreds of times, and had been arrested at least a dozen of them. He loves the archipelago and knows every one of its features: the reef infamous for its resident 14-foot tiger shark; the self-devouring, left-breaking slab that he's never seen surfed; the ruined landing where he says escaped inmates turned on one another in hunger and fought to the death.

And our final day, we were gifted with a single session of offshore, head-high conditions. Five days, $12,000, and the prospect of a trespass rap came down to 90 minutes of roping right reef surf. One takes what one gets—here more than almost anywhere.

Not much has changed at the Marías. Risk and expense. Long runs to fickle prospects. The chance to wallow in astounding wilderness and beauty. You have to take the bone in your teeth. But change is on the wing. A major hotel concession has been granted, flying under a flag of convenience: ecotourism. There might come a time when anyone can venture unimpeded to fish the waters, surf the waves, and marinate, Albino-like, in the glory of the untrodden foreshore. In the meanwhile, the vines lay claim to the old cells, the jungle doing its best to return to the time before any of us showed up.

Isla de Cedros:

An Abecedarian

Handbook

From *The Bight*, Volume 2, Number 1, 2018

A is for Adrian Ojeda, co-founder of the island's original pure fishing lodge, Cedros Adventures. A Baja Norteño, Adrian's background as a tuna-spotting pilot gives him a huge leg up in the category of actionable fish dope. He has low-buzzed every reef, ridge, and kelp bed in the Vizcaíno bight. Hell, he's doing it right now. He knows every contour of Isla Cedros and, along with co-founder Tom Greene, established the Cedros Adventures compound on a raw, oceanfront bluff overlooking the town of Pueblo Cedros. Ojeda is known to feed new arrivals hand-selected cuts of grass-fed Sonoran beef from his secret Ensenadan butcher—delivered same day via his private plane.

B is for beer. As in cartons of iced, sweating cans of Tecate and Modelo Especial. Working-class *claras* built for thirst-quenching in quantities that would invite an ATF Waco action in less civilized latitudes. You load up at a stand-alone liquor store called— what else—"La Panga." Can't miss it. It's right down the hill from the rehab center. Seriously. They have all three flavors of tequila too: *añejo* (older gents really like this caramel-tinged, oaked-out stuff); *joven* (raw, non-aged squeezings with every ounce of agave bite front and center); *reposado* (or "rested," the perfect balance to every cell of my body, excepting my primary biliary duct).

C is for calico bass. The Isla Cedros resource is utterly ridiculous. You can have a banner day and not even need a neon-green nylon jersey festooned with sponsor logos. Nothing can really prepare you for the savagery the big checkers levy. Random acts of lure-jacking and straight-up cannibalism are daily—*hourly*—occurrences at Cedros. Have you ever seen a legitimate foamer of calico bass, not a stinking one of them under four pounds? Piled-up, ass-nipping, surface psychosis? Being too young to have fished San Clemente Island in 1948, I hadn't. When they're chewing out of their skulls in such a manner, you could jack-pole them with an 8-o duct taped to a beach-scrounged pink plastic tampon applicator. (I'm sorry, was that wrong?). The backdrop is an endless series of lovely coves on the front side of the *isla*. Each has a name, and the best ones have nicknames. All are aquatic gardens, with water like silver tequila, kelp groves, and barking *lobos del mar* more interested in lazing on the rocks than killing your fish. Mostly. If this was an island off LA, the water would be bristling with thousands of buoy sticks. But this is an island off central Baja. Hell, there aren't even any *regular* sticks.

D is for Delicados Ovalados. They're cigarettes. Those dumbass things that kill you. Or worse. Delicados are about a dollar a pack, oval-shaped, unfiltered, and have a touch of sugar at the business end. In Baja, they qualify as dessert. One will do you less harm than a Dorito. And, as with Doritos, no one stops at one. This publication, along with the Surgeon General, explicitly recommends against the torching of Delicado Ovalados.

E is for El Cipres Airport in Ensenada, your embarkation point. Nominally, it's a Mexican Air Force base, but it also has scheduled flights to Cedros, Guerrero Negro, and Bahía Tortugas. It's hidden behind a windrow south of the city proper. You've passed it dozens of times but have probably never entered the gate. Opposite from the *The Lost Weekend*-looking El Joker motel.

F is for *frenos*. *Frenos* is Spanish for "brakes." When an attractive woman walks down the Cedros *malecón*, you say, "*Hay que curvas—y yo sin frenos.*" Under your breath, of course. Unless you want to get pounded like a Haliotis (see H) by her brothers.

G is for grr or grand. *Un mil*. It's how much money you win if you cop the coveted Primer Lugar Trophy in the annual Torneo de Pesca Jurel (see J). In pesos, that's over 15,000 clams. If you're on the island during this event, sign up—even if competitive fishing is against your religion. You might get paired up with a stone-faced killer like Lalo, a *panguero* who has put anglers on the winning fish year after year. The Torneo is when the entire town turns into an orgy of yellowtail. The whole place shuts down for the weekend, and La Panga (see B) tests its very foundation with mammoth deliveries of pilsen. There are brass bands and ranchero groups. Kids engaging in hand-to-hand bottle rocket combat. *Jureles* butchered in a cold-hearted manner, the chunks sprinted up to giant mesquite-fuelled *barbacoas*. The *policía* turn a blind eye to all but the most egregious offenses. It's kind of like the Bisbee in Cabo. In 1936.

H is for Haliotis aka *abulón* aka abalone. Pueblo Cedros is a fishing town sharing in the ups and downs of the Pescadores Nacionales de Abulón co-op. In the fall, lobster augments the town's export. Most of the ab is processed, pressure cooked, and canned for both the foreign and national markets. If your paycheck does not depend upon such commerce, pressure cooking of the succulent mollusk is an obscenity. Everyone knows you cut them into steaks, pound them with some vulgar instrument, dip them in egg, drag them through crushed Waverly Wafers, and fry them in peanut oil. With an ass-pocket pint of *reposado* and maybe a Delicado Ovalado.

I is for *isla*. That means "island." And it's perhaps the most unique component of the Cedros experience. Because you can't drive there in a pickup truck, 99 percent of the fishermen visiting Baja never make it to Cedros. There are less of "us" there. Not that "us" are all that bad. It's just that there are too many of "us." And a measurable component of "us" are dipshits. I have data for this. The Dewey Channel between Punta Eugenia and Isla Cedros works like a semi-permeable membrane. A dipshit filter, you might call it. If someone puts in the effort to get to Cedros, their motives are generally pure. They want to engage with the warm and welcoming people of the town. They want to take a few fish and release about a thousand more. They want to go to bed early, too tired to finish a single chapter of their book. They want to get up at gray. They want to eat like barbarians. That's it. *Islas* are good for this.

J is for *jurel*, Spanish for "yellowtail." As you've heard, they grow them big here. A standard-issue Cedros yellow is around 30 pounds. Forties aren't uncommon. Fifties raise eyebrows, but it's not like the banks and government offices close. The most common way to catch them is via the slow-troll. This starts with making macks and Spanish macks hard against the hull of a salt barge. Pin one on a big hook. Fish rope. Like 50 pound, minimum. Minimum. Fish out of gear, thumb-pinning the spool to maintain distance while the *panguero* boxes a likely nearshore zone. At Cedros, nearshore can mean 10 yards off the sand at El Morro. When you get picked up, count to at least four. That's about 15 percent of a Delicado Ovalado. Let them enjoy their last meal. Okay, now slam it in gear and turn the handle. What, it won't turn? *Bienvenidos a Cedros, pariente.*

K is baseball shorthand for strikeout. The Cedros co-op has a team called the Bufeos, or "Killer Whales." They play in an intramural league and kick much ass. Their pitchers, raised on canned snails and stingray *machaca*, throw fastballs that look like they come out of a firehose. The various co-op towns of the Vizcaíno Peninsula have baseball teams, competing against each other in a league. There are no Mets or Blue Jays or Phillies. No, they have bitchin' names like the Ostioneros, the Pescadores, and the Navegadores. The best way to watch one of these games is on horseback or muleback behind the oceanview outfield fence with a Tecate. The whole town attends. You'll be a curiosity, but far from unwelcome.

L is for Lalo. He's one of the captains at Cedros Adventures. He's small in stature but has a huge appetite for putting anglers on personal-best *jureles*. His other favorite thing to do is to catch bomber calicos on the plug. He is good at it. In fact, if you're over 50 you'd call him a "stick." If you're under 50 you'd say he was "sick." If you're Mexicano, you'd say he was *buen piloto*. You could say this about nearly all the *pangueros* on Cedros. But Lalo is a straight-up osprey.

L(2) is for Lomotil™. That's what you buy at the pharmacy if you have *chorro*. And you might. *Chorro* is the Spanish word for "jet."

The locals use it for just about anything that squirts. Mussels are called *chorros*. *Chorro* is also when you suffer foodborne distress, blow an O-ring, and outrage the island with your atomized product. For the love of god, keep some Lomotil™ in your dopp kit.

M is for Mitsubishi Corporation. They run the salt operation at El Morro in joint effort with the Mexican government. Salt is lightered over from the evaporation flats of Guerrero Negro. Freighters can't get into the shallow lagoon there, so they pick it up at Cedros. The barges are offloaded by a scoop conveyor, where the raw salt is mounded into blinding white mountains. Gulls sit on these mountains and crap all over them. They must have a way of refining this guano out—a guy with tweezers or something. Next, a Rube Goldberg-looking device shuttles the salt onto freighters bound for Seattle and Yokohama. The Japanese employees on the freighters scurry around in jumpsuits and powder-blue helmets, making them look like the national guardsmen in *Godzilla*. Some of them catch yellowtail from the deck of the docked freighters.

N is for *nublina*. That's "fog." The mountains are often obscured by a thick layer of the stuff. This is a good time to talk about cedars, the tree the island is named for. There are no cedars on Cedros. Some folks think the Spanish explorers found cedar driftwood, deducing that it must have come from the trees they saw on the ridges. Others think that, being sailors, they didn't know a cedar from a flagpole. Regardless, the trees you see on the mountaintops are juniper and Monterey pine. Since rain is infrequent, much of the island's plant life has adapted to suck out *agua de nublina*: airborne fog water. So, the non-cedars of Cedros drink fog.

O is for "Oh shit." That's what suckas say when they realize that the bar girls in Punta Morro are actually dudes. If there is a better argument for monogamy, I haven't heard it.

P is for *posole*. The gals at Cedros Adventures make the best *posole* in the world. While it is widely believed that the finest cuisine in Mexico comes from Puebla—sort of like Lyon in France and San Sebastián in Spain—the *posole* of Cedros might be the exception proving the rule. *Posole* is, of course, an outrageous red-hell broth studded with hominy, (often) pork, and guajillo chiles, garnished with a sliced avocado, dried Mexican oregano, and a dollop of crema. When you sit down to the table after a full day's fishing and they say dinner is soup, you could be excused for looking crestfallen. That's because you've never had Cedros *posole*. By the end of the trip, you'd gladly fling a double tomahawk to the raccoons in exchange for another bowl of the stuff.

Q is for *quiquiriqui* or *kikiriki*. That's Spanish for "cock-a-doodle-doo." Pueblo Cedros is infested with roosters. They are the crackheads of the animal kingdom and are at their absolute, peaking best when you are in your deepest sleep. They time their piercing mating screams for the precise moment you reach clinical REM. That's why you stay at the lodge on the bluff (see A) instead of in the heart of town.

R is for *reposo*. Also known as "siesta". Or, if in the company of Sinaloans, a *coyotito*. All older, higher cultures enjoy an afternoon nap. Most fishermen arrive so amped up that they're chewing their own arms off. They think the only way for a trip to dollar out is if they're fishing every minute from dawn to dark. On at least one day of your visit to Cedros, come in for lunch, have an hour or two *reposo*, then fish the glass-off. That's luxury, Tex.

S is for surface iron. While slow-trolling is the fail-safe, you're hoping for bird schools. The fish are not picky. Forget what you've learned about offset hips. Deep-six that wounded soldier you got your personal best on back home. When they're chewing up in the roof of the column, it doesn't matter.

T is for tackle. You don't need as much as you think. Three outfits will do: a slow-troll bait setup—preferably with a two-speed reel; a jig stick for propelling the plug (see S). Use one of these as your yoyo device as needed. Your third rig wants to be a stout bass outfit rigged kelp-cutter style (65-pound braid to 50-pound fluoro leader). Forget something or just traveling light? Jeff Mariani's Cedros Tackle has you handled. This being fishing, some cats roll in with about 300 line-feet of rolled fiberglass and composites. Both ways work. One is less hassle.

U is for Francisco de Ulloa (pronounced "oo-YO-ah"). He "discovered" and named Isla de Cedros in 1539. He was on a private exploration funded by his *socio*, Hernán Cortés. Trying for weeks to push north against the prevailing winds, Ulloa finally called it quits. Of course, he might have just been hanging out for the *posole*. He eventually headed back toward Spain.

V is for the incomparable Valle de los Cirios. The Cirios coast is due east of the island. You'll see the sun come up over its mountains from Cedros. There are a couple of shark camps on that shore. They make balls-out, 60-mile runs to longline the island's north point. These cats are semi-*desperado* and not to be messed with for a variety of reasons. Sometimes sharking isn't the only game they run.

W is for wide open. Crazed. Without *frenos*. Biting pink plastic tampon applicators. Like, the best calico fishing you have ever seen in your life. All hyperbole aside, Cedros bassing is the sickest thing around. *Machin*. As in, close this print artifact, boot up your device, log on to Cedros Adventures, and book a trip.

X... I got nothin'.

Y is for yellowtail. That's what the long-rangers call *jurel*. When panga fishing Cedros, you'll occasionally see big, beautiful craft from San Diego steaming through the channel between El Morro and Isla Natividad. The *Red Rooster*, the *Royal Star*, the *Intrepid*, the *Independence*. Et cetera. They're putting their clients on the same thing you're after: gross, shouldered-out yellows. Long-ranging is a good way to see the waters around Cedros, but never land on the island itself. You should probably try it both ways to figure out which you prefer.

Z is for Zam-Mar. Before the lodges went in, that's where you stayed if you were on Cedros. It's a simple hotel in downtown Pueblo Cedros. They'll feed you. They have a boat. They also have roosters. Some hardcore guys drive from Alta California to Punta Eugenia, get on a panga, and run the channel to the island. They invariably stay at Zam-Mar. There is no wrong way to visit the island. Zam-Mar has its fans.

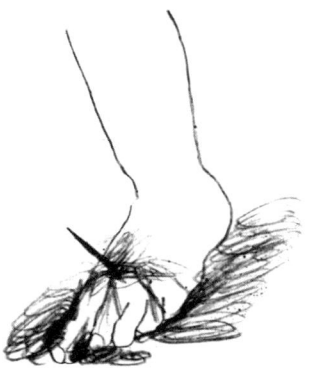

Finisterra

Drunk and disorderly in its modern iteration, Cabo San Lucas is a tough place to love. A hustler's port. A tourist plantation. Vegas-by-the-sea. Divorce Beach remains its most dangerous addiction.

From *The Surfer's Journal*, Volume 24, Number 5, 2015

•

If you've been to Cabo, you've seen El Arco, rife with geologic charisma. Like a widow-maker heart attack, it's where the western edge of North America seized up in one grand *mal* episode, rose to full height, then plunged face-first into the depths.

Immediately offshore, the ocean loses its floor, free falling thousands of feet to the benthic abyss. It stays that way clear to Antarctica. With no continental shelf tapping the brakes, pelagic swells slam the Cape. They arrive pinned in fifth gear, seemingly outraged at the presence of land.

Tucked on the weather side of the Arch lies Divorce Beach, 100 yards of sable-gold sand, a steep berm, and a horror-show shoredump. The waves, even at 2 feet, are grotesque. Some specialists come to Cabo for this very spot. Skimboarders mostly. Bodyboarders. The odd stand-up surfer—usually hammo'd on rum. Like its cousins Keiki and Waimea shorebreaks on the North Shore and Wedge in Newport Beach, Divorce is all about condensed power. Like any heavy whomp spot, one's only hope is to briefly occupy that transition between flat and vertical while potential dismemberment lobs overhead.

I first saw Cabo San Lucas in 1980. I was lucky enough to approach it from sea, on a ferry from Jalisco. Sailing toward the bay, we raised the Sierra La Laguna first, then the sharp definition of the Cape. There were three or four low-rise hotels—the Hacienda, the Mar de Cortez, the Solmar, and an edifice named for Land's End, the Finisterra. A couple of liquor stores and restaurants. A rotisserie chicken joint of the type found near all Mexican bus stations. A fish cannery. My pal and me, lugging backpacks and boards, were in the clubhouse turn on a month-long, street-level surf trip through Sinaloa and Nayarit. The Tip felt like a small homecoming. The bugs, the smoldering smudge pots, the punishing humidity of the mainland—all left behind. Here the air was as dry as a finger snap. Clear, clean swell was in evidence. We decided to stay awhile, exploring the sporadically visited points farther up the gulf.

Subsequent trips taught us well: Flat days were for the back side of Lover's Beach. With a single kick, we'd launch in where the side wave died, free falling into short drainers, the sandstone sea stacks framed in green—a last, fleeting recollection before another near concussion. Whomp heaven. On days with any swell at all, it quickly outpaced our interest and abilities. Waves sucked below sea level, loading up impossibly before *ka-whumping* in beach-shaking explosions. Heinous currents bloomed after sets, ripping millions of gallons of water into the rocks. Getting back in became a real issue.

Since those pilsner-tinged days of yore, the town has grown into a city. A sort of favela now climbs the alluvial plain to the north. There's a massive Costco, a Home Depot, a Wal-Mart. The waterfront is unrecognizable, groaning under the load of hundreds of beer mills, kitsch shops, clip joints, and *ficha* bars. Cruise-ship Canadians, socks pulled high and tight, walk stunned through the crush. Corners are controlled by bindle slingers with cell phones and bleached-tipped haircuts, speed-rapping their pitches: "Blow…Weed…Oxy…" Directly across the street, bored-looking Federal Gendarmerie, Chilangos from the DF, ignore the retailing. Someone has this town on lock, and it ain't the Rosicrucians.

I'm here bright and early to meet Drew Peace. We'll call him the mayor of Lover's Beach. He's lived here all of his life, excepting the four years he spent *al otro lado* copping a degree from SDSU. His dad, a spearfisherman, raised him in an apartment over the Giggling Marlin. So he got an eyeful. He also got street smart, bilingual, and endlessly connected. Peace worked every carny game in town, hustling boat rides, fishing trips, and custom student tours, whereby planeloads of G-strung co-eds would be delivered right into his loving and respectful care. Every non-working hour was spent at Lover's. Peace developed a kink for the place. It was the closest legal kick to his home. Soon, he was as comfortable carving giant whomp on his skimboard as any professional visitor. He earned a name in that core little side current of surfing.

I liked him instantly. I was staying with an expat pal in nearby Todos Santos, and Peace had offered to decode the modern scene from a subterranean perspective. "This place is a circus, you have to understand that," he said, needlessly. He was driving us through downtown in his corroded little truck. "Everybody comes here: LA people, Euros, fishermen, rich Mexicans, not-so-rich Mexicans... If I didn't have Lover's, it'd be tough."

I've seen and heard that story before. It's obvious just watching him drive, his eyes darting, looking for tells. He's addicted to the whole of it. Mexican cacophony and color. The smells and street pageantry. The louche scam of it all. To be 29, a dual citizen, and with endless ways to earn gray-market coin without missing a surf? Most would go down in flames inside a year. Peace has his head screwed on, but with enough play in the threads to take occasional advantage.

"So the beach, yeah..." He scrounges a hidden parking spot in the marina. "It's heavy for sure. They don't even report how many people die there each year." He's right. Drive-by research shows only a handful of recent deaths at Lover's according to the US Department of State.

We're walking to the dock to jump on a friend's panga, squeezed in next to some visitors from Vancouver. Tom Wolfe's "gray panthers." Peace says, "You know the deal. People on damp sand, oblivious, then a wave bowls them over and sucks them into the impact zone." Osterized, sometimes not found for days. Sometimes never found.

We nose in on the harbor side of Lover's, and I see what's come of the place. The demographics tell the story: Indonesian stewards in nylon briefs, on break from the cruise ship anchored nearby. Sunburned bachelorettes popping their morning beers, debauched but rallying. A couple of shredded brothers from Montreal with plastic Mardi Gras cups. All latent cannon fodder for the waves, blue and tempting over the berm on the ocean side.

Marching us to the back side of the Cape, Peace continues: "The beer vendors have all the stories and they take care of the beach. They pick up trash, yell at tourists who are putting themselves at risk." Peace slaps five with a sun-fried *vendedor* and stabs his thin board into the sand. The waves are small, but Land's End creates a violent little lineup of its own volition. The nearshore abruptness, the current flooding downhill, the tide—it lifts your self-preservation hackles, roaching the hair on the back of your neck. Eighty yards from the harbor side, it's devoid of humanity. A flop, then a turn, then a river of Galapagos pelicans carves around the point. High above, a *pirata*, or frigatebird, spins on a hot updraft, looking for an unsuspecting gull to hijack. Like the Eiffel Tower-hating Parisian who dined in its restaurant every day, we're in Cabo but we don't have to look at it.

"The worst story," Peace says, "happened about 10 years ago. A guy from Hollywood was standing on the beach with his two kids. A big finger of water rocketed up the berm and snatched the older kid. The guy freaked and chased him into the water. Couldn't get to him. While this was going on another wave blasted up the beach and took the other kid. Just a worst-case scenario. He lost them both."

The deeply cusped beach speaks to heavy swell days, defying today's barely there conditions. A young Mexican sprints down the beach toward us, rail thin, all teeth and elbows. "That's Bullo Nazario," Peace says. "He used to sell chicle on a corner in town. We took him under our wing." Peace hooked him up with small product sponsorships and coached him to such a point that he's now one of the best skimboarders in the world. Awash in size 26 trunks, Bullo sprints into the water, throws his board, chips in on the sidewash, and launches into, I don't know, a double-grab Salchow or something.

Peace checks his watch, dons his Elvis shades, and whistles our boat over. Moments later, we're idling past massive, helicopter-bedecked megayachts. Only a few hundred feet from the quay, no land is in evidence. It's all stucco and touts, a machine designed to pull C-notes from the pockets of squares. Yet in a wave-riding world gone hopelessly mainstream, and in a venue as spirit bereft as latter-day Cabo, Peace has carved out a legit surfing life. On-the-fly street smarts and the reading of warping shorepound are complementary hues. And Peace, already staging for his next move, is nothing if not a colorist.

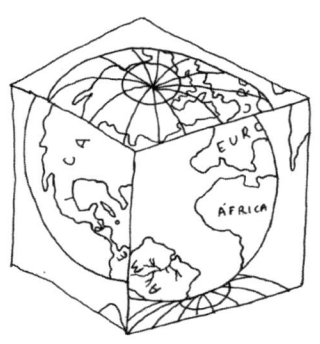

26.56.96: A Basque Continuum

From *Super X Media Combine*, 2003

•

Two thousand pounds of snot-flinging force *majeure* explodes from behind a wooden door and gores a young man in the rectum, flinging him backward with a twitch of the shoulders. The second animal uses the crumpled body for traction, then sprints down the cobbled alley in pursuit of a few score of white-clad Basques. Down the line, a shepherd swings on the face of a participant with a wooden switch, enforcing the "no taunting" rule. After the bulls have been hustled into the ring for the afternoon's corrida, a commercial water cannon cruises the route, hosing the accumulation of blood, dung, wine bottles, and drunkards into the plaza for collection.

Tyler Hatzikian and Mitch Abshere, a pair of throwback longboard surfers from California, observe. They only observe in deference to custom, and the fact that the running is held in somber esteem by the villagers. It would be a coarse desecration to simply jump in and join the fray. While it's party time at the Festival de San Fermín, and Pamplona still throws down, the locals have slim regard for the uninformed.

Who would have predicted that California surf culture, at less than 80 years old, would form a flat-scar suture with that of the Basque people, polished by 3,000 years and counting? Pamplona and its Running of the Bulls earned acclaim through Ernesto Hemingway's *Fiesta* (released as *The Sun Also Rises* in the US) back in '26. During the filming of the screen version in '56, writer Peter Viertel brought Los Angeles surf culture to Biarritz via his wooden Velzy-Jacobs Malibu board. Frenchmen Joel de Rosnay and Jo Maratz fired up the local scene. The surf synergy continued when riders Billy Hamilton, Mark Martinson, and Keith Paull surfed at La Barre, lending a measure of Euro-cool to Jim Freeman and Greg MacGillivray's film work. The Basque country of the Spanish-French border has held a place in surf lore ever since.

The waves and overall zeitgeist of the Pays Basque (from Hossegor in southern France to Mundaka in northern Spain) remain relatively unchanged. The *vin et pain* program still provides sustenance, while the milky-green sand peaks nourish the imagination. To arrive in the Gucci-Napoleonic hamlet of Biarritz with a boat-cloth-glassed step deck, a month at your disposal, and a pocketful of francs is to backpedal in time. Yet a reference point is required for all accurate dead reckoning.

In the not-so-way back, the Steakhouse in Biarritz was the de rigueur hang for what "Frail Dale" Davis called "The Golden Breed." Now it's Le Surf, a bar on the strand at La Côte Basque. Here you'll find what you seek, be it news of a freshly spawned sandbar at Zarautz or a crisply rolled Lebanese/*tabac* burrito. Delve into the latter-day fall of Rome that is the Playboy Club. Hit the *supermarché* for Bordeaux and fromage. Mind and satchel charged, you're well-advised to proceed north or south, toward hollower pastures.

North takes you to Anglet and Bayonne, a series of jetty breaks and mid-tide sandbanks. South sends you to Guéthary, Saint-Jean-de-Luz, San Sebastián, and on down through the Spanish frontier to Mundaka. You're now in the heart of it, the Pays Basque, home of the oldest language in the world, incredible rivermouths, justifiably proud men, and stunning, impeccably postured women. Ernesto did the unthinkable by placing the hero of *Fiesta*, Jake Barnes, a groin-damaged soldier, in perhaps the most fertile crescent of feminine beauty on the sphere. You, being healthy, will revel.

Simple laws of travel hold well here. The wise do just enough homework to give depth, but not enough to make things predictable. Those down with Picasso, the Spanish Civil War, Hemingway, and the plight of the Basques pull more than those flying dull. Don't crumple during flat spells. Tighten up the program with runs into the mountains, to Pamplona, and to the hill villages.

The people of the Pays Basque? Living in an XL style is the order of any given day, with priority given largely to sport. Every Basque town has a pelota court, where wagers are placed on hand and basket-driven ball games. Fiesta is spent quaffing alcoholic cider and local wine, with heaping plates of paella, *gambas al ajillo*, and lamb brochettes. More extreme elements of the Basque culture include a radical revolutionary fringe, given to bombings, riots, and the like. Stay away from any overt gatherings of the Guardia Civil, the Spanish civil/rural guard. They're occasionally the targets of homespun incendiary devices.

Since time immemorial, Spain has been a seafaring nation, and the Basque Coast is peppered with oceanfront villages: Guipúzcoa, Bakio, and Sopelana all have surf scenarios worth investigating. The enlightened avoid the overrun locales in favor of keyhole bays and hidden reefs. Choreographic clues lifted from the blood-stained dirt of the bull ring can be translated into a wet medium in the quiet of a deserted bay. Under such conditions, you may find yourself wondering, perhaps, if it's '26…'56… or '96. And it just won't matter. The rolling hills and waves of the

Pays Basque will remain long after your own corporeal self is reduced to so much smoke and ash. Euskadi.

The Other Sea of Cortez

Spare a thought for Sonora—and San Carlos-style yellowtail jigging.

From *The Bight*, Volume 3, Number 2, 2019

•

Fernando Almada marks yellows near the bottom at 100 feet, kicks into neutral, and deep-sixes a foot-long knife jig to the basement. On his fourth quick pitch-and-lift, things come tight violently. The headshakes transmit into his body like he's being electrocuted. It's a yoyo slam turned to 11. Why? His outfit weighs about 15 ounces.

After a standard drag-burning *jurel* run, the fish slows. Almada's flimsy slow-pitch rod lacks the spine to horse the fish in a traditional manner, so he stabs the tip into the water, straight winching until he gains real ground with a series of high-sticking, noodled-out pump-and-grinds. Working the fish to leader, he leans over and hoists it up by the jig.

The first time you see hybrid jigging, it can look a little flamboyant: one wind (or "pitch"), one lift, done at varying rates of speed. You ask yourself the obvious question: Are they getting bit more than they would with typical yoyo gear? On this day, it's obvious. Almada is wrecking shop. Granted, these are teen-grade fish, but the tackle—and the technique—are clearly up to the task. Where eliciting bites is concerned, properly animated jigs work like sorcery. Indeed, the concept can make the standard 40N or two-speed reel and thick-walled yoyo stick seem like archaic overkill.

Almada yoyo'd for deep yellows for decades, but this new mode—using slow-pitch gear with jigs normally used for the more angle-frenetic speed jigging—has ruined him for any other approach.

"It's a total addiction," Almada says. "I'll do this every day until my arms fall off."

His method is a hybrid solution specifically designed for his waters in Sonora, Mexico, and it's been optimized for the most beloved species from the SoCal Bight to the Cortés—the California yellowtail. Will Californians ever embrace the mode or the waters in which it was born? Only if we get off our Baja obsession. Good luck with that.

Looking off to the sunrise from Baja's eastern shore, we give little thought to continental Mexico. Easier to focus on the job at hand, nursing coffees and tying on sabikis. There's work to be done right here. Sonora? Sinaloa? They might as well be Central American nations, detached as they are from SoCal fishing consciousness. After all, we have a lifetime punch list to investigate on the Mar de Cortés: Gonzaga, Bahía de los Ángeles, San Francisquito, Mulegé, Loreto, and on down until the peninsula gets skinny.

Yes, to the bulk of Californian fishermen, the mainland side of Mexico might as well start at Mazatlán and end at Puerto Vallarta, destinations associated with resorts, tourists, and those lavishly tipping Canadians. (I kid. We love our Canuck cousins.) But doesn't that leave half of the Cortés unspoken for? Most Baja bush vets know the western Cortés down to a granular level. You'll have a harder time finding folks with Yaqui knowledge. And while most anglers have heard of Rocky Point, Kino Bay, and San Carlos/Guaymas, few of us actually go there.

Not surprisingly, these coastal-desert waypoints while away in obscurity, the victims of challenging access. Sure, Arizonans enjoy easy toll road cruising on Mexico 15, and the region's handful of coastal holiday towns are well-loved by

Mexican travelers. But man, guys with a hankering for Baja the way it used to be might consider, well, getting out of Baja. To some, that will sound like heresy. Let's unpack that.

The key to the whole program is TIJ, with a side of CBX. That's using the modern and streamlined Tijuana airport, accessed via the Cross Border Xpress bridge. (My friends have long tired of me touting the program. Sorry: Based on ease, cleanliness, and civility, Tijuana dunks on stateside airports.) From there, it's a one-hour flight to Hermosillo and another hour to San Carlos via a $60 Uber. Lodging, meals, and bars abound. Punch in a local taxi driver's WhatsApp number and your transport needs are met. Now it's time to get out to meet Sonora.

The state has some unique and distinguishing characteristics. Giant, crepe-like flour tortillas. Fork-tender, grass-fed beef. Comparatively tall, light-skinned natives. And an utter dearth of gringos. I like that. But I like seeing the pueblo making some scratch even more. That's where the Arizonans come in. They install themselves each December and don't decamp until Easter. For San Carlos—indeed, for the greater Guaymas area—they provide a welcome breeze of green.

For AZers as well as anyone else, the baseline appeal of the coastline is obvious. Picture the mesas, peaks, and buttes of Sedona or Monument Valley. Now plunge them into the sea. Beyond that, it's a richly verdant desert, as one might see in central Baja only immediately after a rain. Like Tucson's Catalina Mountains compared to, say, Borrego Springs.

The shoreline is geographically tortured, ripped with flash-dried volcanic headlands and deep, fjord-like coves. Beaches are occasional but snow-blind white. A handful of islands give visual interest, all lorded over by Tetekawi, the twin-peaked landmark predictably named "Goat Tits" by the Yaquis. The coast has the easily appreciated charisma of Baja's Las Animas or Ensenada Blanca.

The harbor sets the place apart. Taking the moniker "Hurricane Hole" to an extreme, the modern little marina is tucked like a pearl protected by an impenetrable clamshell. San Carlos is lightly commercialized, with none of the garish *mierda* one finds across the pond in thrice-overbuilt Cabo San Lucas. That effect is mimicked by the small, neatly effective sportfishing fleet. Along with the aforementioned Almada, highly referenced captains like Abel Anaya, an absolute master of the circle-hooked ballyhoo striped marlin game, are at your service. There's a hotel, some condos, a handful of restaurants geared to gringo sensibilities, and a fuel dock. It's an "everything you need and nothing you don't" kind of place.

It's also where Almada—a Guaymas resident—hangs his tackle-shop shingle, spitting distance from his center-console 'Cat. Such twin hulls are common in these parts. Despite the overwhelming popularity of traditional pangas throughout Mexico, 21- and 26-foot SeaCats are a cult classic here. Like jigging, it's all about regional application.

"Over the years, more and more 'Cats have shown up," says Almada. "After riding the short-period chop we have here, they're such a great ride. Smooth and dry! For our conditions, once you go 'Cat you'll never go back."

Onboard, the widely placed twin 150s allow him to spin the boat on its heels in not much more than a boat length. Once underway, the ride speaks for itself. Indeed, the local fleet of SeaCats is one of San Carlos' many surprising pleasures. Having joined Almada to go to school on his technique, my pal and me take in the landscape. Heading north past a go-to *jurel* spot called Tordilla, Almada balls it up-coast for La Manga. It's a perfect September morning. The appeal of fishing barefoot, shirtless, with a one-pound rig is a no-brainer. As we slide onto his mark, Almada talks about the genesis of San Carlos jigging.

"A friend, Craig Collins, used to be a deckhand on the San Diego long-range boats," says Almada. "He was the one who turned my attention toward jigging. I remember taking him out once, we started trolling—like we did all the time back then for yellows—and then he asked me to stop so he could jig. His fishing nickname was actually 'Iron Man.' I remember it as if it happened yesterday: He caught four nice *jurel* and I just could not stop thinking, *That sure looks like a lot more fun than trolling*. I remember getting home and immediately looking all over the internet for jigging info. I got a couple of jigging reels, tried it myself with no luck, and thought, *This sucks*.

"The very next time Craig was in town he let me use one of his setups. I landed my first fish on a jig and I was hooked. Then I found a video of some Japanese guys using a knife jig. I ordered some and had them delivered to Craig's house in AZ. On his next trip to SC, he brought them down and we both looked at the jig with the hooks on top and thought, *This is never going to work*. It only took me a couple of drops to figure out how wrong we were. After a few trips, the knife-style jigs started outfishing the conventional iron. We still have yoyo iron and use them from time to time—works as good as ever—but the new style of jigging seems to work better for us. Or maybe [it's just more fun]."

Almada notes some likely worms on the meter and has us drop. He outfits interested clients with a full complement of rigs, and I drew a ramen-thin Tsunami slow-jig rod with a tiny Maxel conventional reel. A 150-gram, slider-style jig with a single-assist hood speeds its way to bottom. *Now what*, I wonder. *Just start spazzing?* He explains it easy as pie: "Wind once. When the tip rebounds, do it again. That's it." By the third drop, it feels natural. He has us increasing the pace but stopping well short of yoyo speed. And yeah, that's when we get tripled. Total "Hollywood can't make it up" shit. All three of us are giggling like schoolgirls.

"I told you," Almada says. "Yoyo-ing with a 6080 jig stick, my shoulder and back would kill me. Using the 6'6", 6'8", and even 7' slow-pitch rods, it got pretty much effortless. They are so sensitive, you can feel when your jig is swimming up with the right action. That's when the bites start happening. We also went from high-speed reels to regular-speed reels or slow-speed reels. A steady rhythm is way more important than raw speed. Of course, there are days that the faster the better, but the same is true the other way around."

Within an hour or so, we limit out on teener yellows. They're bigger than firecrackers—call them M-80s—but small enough to embolden my next question: "How do these bendy Okinawan Gobi killers do with a legit mossback?" Almada answers that his best slow-pitch fish was a 30—at the top end for yellowtail in the area. Regardless of target, he employs a proven system of terminal tackle.

"I prefer long, skinny jigs," says Almada. "I like fluoro leaders, and I never go bigger than my main line—if I use 40 pound, I go with 40-pound fluoro or less. I spool my reels from bottom to top with braid and use a six- to eight-foot leader. I never use a swivel or snap on my setups. I tie a Sebile or FG knot to join braid and leader, then keep it simple with a Palomar knot to tie on my jig. I prefer to use figure-eight rings to avoid the sharp end of the split ring chipping away at my knot. I am a charter guy so I am not too picky about hooks—whatever I have available."

Almada is as fish-pumped as anyone you'd care to meet. With none of us in the mood for trolling, he offers a gunkhole passage and secret-spot tour. "Here's a place for surface iron cabrilla. There's a headland where the locals slay yellows right off the rocks. Check out this spot where guys knock out 15-pound sea bass off the sand." By the time we motor, we have a working knowledge of San Carlos' inshore riches.

By week's end, we've hammered yellows relentlessly, shorepounded *toritos*, bonitos, and *gallitos* by the dozen on 10-pound mono, low-profile baitcasters, and travel rods, and achieved "intermediate" jigging status. We've seen one other stateside fisherman. The locals are relaxed, unjaded, and happy to leave you alone. Every now and then, the landside visuals jump out and surprise us. The lager is cheap, plentiful, and ice cold. The Baja effect had our blood pressure down by half on day one. Except, you know, we aren't in Baja.

We arrange an Uber back to the Hermosillo airport, building in two hours for a visit to Asadero El Leñador. Picture your very favorite US steakhouse. Now replace its factory-farmed, feed-lot beef with free-range Angus raised on zacate grass and well water. Grill that ribeye medium rare (*al punto*) on live mesquite, chop it up, and drop it onto a house-made tortilla. Charge three bucks per. That's Sonora. Reason alone to come back. We will.

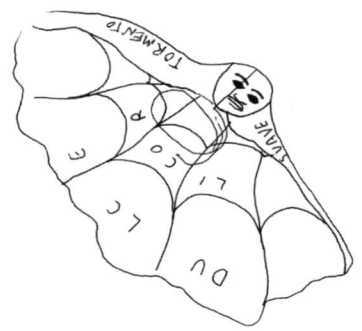

Sucker-Free on the Ruta del Sol

Just say the words and we'll beat the birds down to Acapulco Bay.

•

Two kinds of people travel for beachbreak: big-wave surfers and the crowd-averse. If you're not the air-vest and double-leash-plug sort headed for Zicatela or Tecomán, you're probably cool with head-high, spindrift-addled sandbars. And you might cotton to 82-degree water and a jungle-scented land breeze. Alone.

If hell is indeed other people, these are challenging times to be a near-metropolitan hominid. In this "everyone surfs" epoch—primary venues cheek-to-jowl, secondary zones jugged with commercial camps, third-tier spots infested with surf schools—point and reef options can feel like they're drying up. But there's a play beyond complaining or piling on to the scrum. Sometimes one needs a respite from oversaturation. A damn-the-algorithm hunch. Consider tunneling down to less-obvious plays. Places with dependable, if not world- or even national-class beachbreak. Places with a sidecar of discovery, surprise, and strong odds of surfing with vaguely welcoming locals curious about your very presence. Places like Acapulco.

While a far cry from glory-spot quality, seclusion has its privileges. There's something freeing and surreal to be the only one dragging a board bag through a Mexican coastal air terminal in 2022. The weight of expectation disappears. There's an unstudied feeling. You're no longer party to the most over-examined lifestyle and industry on the stinking orb. You're merely a traveler with some oddly shaped luggage. (Try that on a flight from LAX to Cabo.) And overhead spitters are firing within a kilometer of the taxi stand.

Made internationally famous in the 1950s by Elvis and Sinatra, Acapulco was *the* spot to party during your grandparents' time. When Cap d'Antibes and Gustavia seemed gauche and overplayed, Aca slapped like a fat-bottomed mango dropped from great height. It put Mexico on the jet-set map. The sort of place surfers generally take pains to avoid, sure. But Lord, did it have some intangibles. Topography, music, *vibra*. All still there, and all made decidedly more valuable by the lack of the greater "us." International tourism crashed more than 15 years ago, the result of some extremely ugly mafia flare-ups. It's still a sketchy little city, and you can easily find trouble if you go looking for it in the barrios behind the beaches. This is no place to pursue what Mexicans refer to as *la vagancia*.

Keep to the beaches and you'll find your surfed-out self reveling in the diabolically old-school Hotel Las Brisas, the Boca Chica, or Los Flamingos. Venues perfectly suited to linen-clad treachery—hatching a life-insurance scam or jacking a casino cage. These joints retain the ghosts of capers past, waiting for new hosts. All of those old haute monde haunts have a way of inspiring a touch of larceny.

The susceptible might be better served staying down by Revolcadero. This historically resonant beach south of the city is where Mainland Mexican surfing was born. Before Puerto Escondido was even a gleam, the first national surfers left the swell-bound bay of Aca for the exposed bars stretching toward Oaxaca. Setting up out front of what is now the Pierre Mundo Imperial hotel, a local scene developed. The rivermouth, sheltered by a jungle headland, offered an automat of peaks. Talent burbled to the top, and *veteranos* like "El Campeon" are still proudly cited by the young bucks.

Today, Playa Bonfil—another mile south of Revolcadero—is the modern hub of hardcore surf activity. A few dozen surfers claim it as their local. It's a scruffy stretch of ramadas fronting a clean, stray-dog-patrolled beach. The ramadas open at eight o'clock in the morning or so, serving up *café de olla*, papaya, and *huevos al gusto*. A handful of foreign visitors jungle up in the winter, prime time for Bonfil. Beyond that, there's not a hell of a lot going on.

The neighborhood backing the beach is spotted with markets, shoe-repair shops, and hardware stores. There are also a dozen or so hostelries, ranging from backpacker squats on up to two-storied pool *hotelitos*. A pair of traveling surfers could get by here on 50 bucks (about 1,000 pesos) each a day, no sweat. Just don't count on meeting many fellow hunters. What you can count on is hanging with Aca surfers, who seem especially warm and good-humored. With such light traffic, it almost harks back to California of the mid-'50s, when surfers would pull their cars over and rap out when they saw another wagon with boards hanging out the back. Almost. Mostly, though, one can count on an air of pleasant indifference. When you engage, do it in Spanish—however threadbare. You'll be invited into the shade of a *palapa*, handed something cold or fragrant, and queried about your waves back home. Just don't come in summer.

Local surfers like Chelo Trujillo wait patiently through the hot season, nothing short of Sumerian in the depth of August.

"That's when we drive to [Huatulco]," Chelo says. "It's too big here and just closes out. We wait for big winter swells—like, Waimea swells—to come down to us. Then the beach turns into rights. Hollow, long rights. Not even like a beachbreak."

Checking the sandbars with Chelo in November, one gets a taste of the shoulder season. It feels good. Fair weather, slack winds. The sand has settled from the hurricanes, mixed swell carving out rip channels. A dozen or so local surfers, nearly half of them women and girls, set up on opposing sides of each rip. These aren't hard-hitting barrels of the Pascuales variety. There's some tube riding going on, no doubt, but these are performance waves. Thin-lipped, pitching, curvaceous little benders perfectly suited to straight-up schralping. A touch of tide makes it amenable to noseriding. Something for everyone.

Including Chelo, a prime local product. He lives in a pueblo just inland of Bonfil, but hardly finds that a problem. He's here every day. A grab bag of local sponsors keeps him clothed. Tall, light-footed, and flicky—it would come as a surprise if he weighs 130—he nonetheless keeps his board planted through hard down-carves and bottom turns, artfully finding projection until a barrel presents, which he quickly inhabits. He exits one, prones out to the beach, and trots up to find Arturo Monroy Astudillo watching him from a beachside table.

Arturo is a lifelong surfer in his middle sixties, a stalwart promoter of surfing in Guerrero, and a lighthouse of knowledge regarding the area. Trim, well-spoken, and enthusiastic, his historical recall is as sharp as his boosterism for the young rippers like Chelo. He needs little prodding to relate one of the more compelling stories from Acapulcan surf lore.

"Well, let me begin to tell you about 'El Campeon,'" Arturo says. "Evencio García Bibiano was the best local surfer here by far—a many-time national champion. It happened here during a heat to decide the state champion. One minute he was there, and the next he was gone. Thirty meters from the beach. Judges, lifeguards, spectators—no one saw what happened. He disappeared. His body was never found."

Sucker-Free on the Ruta del Sol

Pointing up the beach to the north, Arturo notes the rivermouth. He says that it's notorious for shark attacks. One of the more horrifying examples occurred "a few years back," when a Japanese surfer and fisherman was hit while wading out to a sandbar. He was never recovered. "El Campeon" Bibiano likely met a similar fate, Arturo says, but he admits that no one knows for sure. No body, no autopsy. No face, no case. Regardless, the state of Guerrero in general and Acapulco in specific has a well-deserved reputation for man-eater-class tigers.

Shark attacks, falling squarely into the "What can you do?" category, don't seem to trouble the Bonfil clique. Indeed, little does.

The crew rallies around Victor Perez's Bonfil Surf Shop. They voyage north and south to famous waypoints and waves you've never heard of. They listen, rapt, to the old boys telling about the sessions of yore. Watching another barrel pleasantly caving in, you're reminded of the gifts of scale. And of appreciation. Beachbreak does that. And, for a surfer, so does Acapulco.

Off the Arroyo

Alonso Macklis traces his lineage to the days of sail. He's also one of the most requested *pangueros* on the East Cape. Join him for a day in his hometown of La Ribera.

From *The Bight*, Volume 1, Number 1, 2017

The original Baja skiffman might have been a coastal Yaqui embarking from the Sonoran foreshore in the early 1900s, blown to Calamajué by a winter norther. He might have been a Cochimí engaged in the treacherous crossing of the Dewey Channel from Punta Eugenia to Isla Cedros off the Pacific Coast. He could well have been an intrepid *marinero* from La Cruz in Nayarit, in one of that town's artisanal single-tree canoas. Whether survival epics or leaps of faith, one thing is certain: That ride across the Mar had to have been a rail clencher.

The bulk of these early ventures were undoubtedly near-shore affairs—doghole passages down current-ripped coastlines. But with each successful mission, the boundaries were pushed. In the Mar de Cortés, early fishermen began to make passages to the islands of the Mar—Tiburón, Ángel de la Guarda, San Marcos.

Small campsites were established along a wind-prescribed trade route. As one might imagine, these haul-outs were associated with freshwater. Brackish esteros were common waypoints, as were those few coastal arroyos with rudimentary wells. Sometimes a hidden *tinaja*, or natural rainwater cistern, was accessed. Some of the camps were inhabited seasonally. Small herb gardens. Sun-bombed stick shelters. A boneyard of tortoise shells.

According to the ebullient—and romantically creative—outdoor writer Ray Cannon, these *vagabundos del mar* spent their lives ghosting around the Mar de Cortés, driven by oar and lateen-rigged sail, drying their catch for *machaca* and selling enough to provision with masa, cooking oil, and cigarettes. Cannon's depiction was told with much artistic license and a sparkle-eyed sense of enchantment that many still feel today: "Just what caused them to take to the sea, none will tell but if they were seeking boundless freedom, they found it. Not only have they escaped all the laws, regulations, and rules imposed by today's society, they have found total release from worries and apprehensions that keep modern men gyrating like addled mice." (*Western Outdoor News*, 1/27/61)

Since that pre-motorized, subsistence-level era, *panguero* culture experienced a predictable evolution rooted in technology and economics, stress and density. First came the plywood-on-frame skiff, then the transformational outboard engine. Next was the global demand for shark liver oil in the mid-century. The introduction of the "World Bank" or "Yamaha" molded hull—almost immediately dubbed a "panga" after its African machete-like profile—was especially dramatic. Pushed far and fast, these efficient, flat-bottomed skiffs carried a huge payload of nets, floats, and marketable catch. The once itinerant *vagabundo* became a co-op gillnetter with a home port and a family.

With the arrival of the first sportfishermen to Baja Sur in the 1950s, a small demand developed for those with local knowledge. Who better to find the seamounts, the deep reefs, the grouper holes than the local turtlers and *totuava* hunters? The *panguero* emerged as the Americano fisherman's friend, his traditional skills suddenly in demand as the sporting world turned its gaze to the "world's biggest fish trap."

Today, the *panguero* evolution leads to Alonso Macklis—and a couple of hundred like him. A commercial handliner and star guide at reference-point lodge Rancho Leonero, Macklis,

63, comes from a long line of fishermen from the nearby town of La Ribera. But his ancestor, a Scot named Macleish, jumped ship in La Paz well over a century ago. Today, the Macleish name is found up and down the peninsula in a variety of spellings, from Alonso's family in La Ribera clear up to Punta Marron on the central Pacific coast. The original Macleish, it would appear, rarely shied away from the chance to lift his kilt. In 2014, his descendant Macklis is happily married—but pure *panguero*.

Predawn on a cool October morning, Macklis loads his vehicle for the washboard run from his home in La Ribera. His destination, as it has been for the last two of his 39 years as a charter captain, is the esteemed Rancho Leonero. He spent 25 years at Spa Buena Vista to the north, and 12 years at Punta Colorado before they closed due to water issues. The five-mile drive is a straight shot down the Camino Costero, a graded hardpan road with the occasional stretch of decomposed granite sand flushed down from the Sierra La Laguna. Indeed, the Arroyo La Ribera is massive, clearly discernible from outer space satellite imagery. This is where a consortium of investors recently cut a new marina. It's the biggest news to hit town since Mexico 1 was paved back in '73. In the author's fifth-grade Spanish, Macklis is asked for his opinion. He changes the subject, instead pointing out the towering mango trees that his grandfather planted in the '30s.

Pulling into the *palo fierros* where the fishermen park their trucks, Macklis swings his tackle over his shoulder to meet the tractor on the beach. The Ranch has a portable pier that can be pushed into the shallows and retrieved when the day is done. In the gray light, it feels like a port town girding for some minor naval invasion. Boats run circles in the morning-sick chop, jockeying for position. Early rising fishermen pace the beach, staring into the thin light for their ride. Macklis is jacked up, cracking jokes, hands waving, searching for the cap he quickly finds on his head. With a leap, he's aboard the *Mosca Magic*. It's a seafoam green Van Diaz Super Panga powered with a recent Yamaha 150 four-stroke. Like the rest of the Rancho pangas, it has a center console, outriggers, a fold-down bimini, and not much else. But as has been proven since the emergence of the form, not much else is truly required. These hulls have raised every fish on offer in the region, a fact not lost on Macklis. He prefers the walkaround functionality of the panga to the larger California flybridge cruisers.

A stop at the bait boat yields a couple of dozen goggle-eyed *caballitos*. Macklis suggests a quick run toward the curve for amberjack. Afterward, he says, it'll be slow-trolling for roosters up against the beach. We voice our preference for inshore species, maybe pompano and sierra to augment the *gallos*. Macklis nods in agreement—then turns the skiff offshore. We keep our traps shut, as only the mentally touched would second-guess his notions. Macklis can't help himself and, like any good charter operator, he knows what we need better than we do.

The boat has a meager electronics pack. There's a VHF radio, but Macklis doesn't care much for chatter. Besides, he knows exactly what to do with the day. He has fished every high spot and crevice between Las Arenas and Destiladeras. If there are fish to be caught, he'll be the one doing it. Besides, he isn't a complete Luddite. He has some trusted spots logged in his GPS. After an hour or so, the deep drops aren't cutting it, so down to the lighthouse we go.

On the way south, Macklis yells at us, "*Las rocas en la marina, recuerdan?*" Yeah, we saw the jetties. "*Aya,*" he says, pointing to the hillside behind Los Barriles. There's a quarry hacked into the slope where the granite trucks rolled. I ask him again: "Is the coming of the marina a good thing?" I'm genuinely curious. He sucks his teeth and quickly answers in the affirmative. He explains the chronic outboard motor thefts at the hands of Sinaloan pirates. He notes that on one occasion the government stepped in and underwrote replacement motors. But the thefts continued. For the commercial fleet, it turned into a tragic opera. Bone tired after a night's fishing, they were forced to drag their boats up the beach and trailer them home, safe from the seaborne *rateros*.

Beyond the newfound security of patrolled slips, revenue will spread through the town, Macklis assures. Stores, marine mechanics, services—all will need employees. The town is poor and jobs are scarce. Yet Macklis claims there are not enough young laborers to support the construction, so hundreds, maybe thousands of workers will have to be imported. That, he says, is how the trouble begins. When the project is complete, the workers remain, now unemployed and strangers to the multi-generational townsfolk of La Ribera. One need only look south, to Los Cabos, to see how that hand plays.

"*Vamos a ver,*" says Macklis, steering his panga between the twin jaws of the new Cabo Riviera Marina. Let's go take a look. "Riviera." Macklis looks for a reaction when he says the word. Perhaps, I suggest, we'll see Brigitte Bardot cavorting. The water is slick and silted, having just been deluged by the trailing edge of Hurricane Odile. Only a sidewalk-narrow channel is navigable. It looks like one of dozens of stillborn Baja boondoggles, a maritime ghost town for the time being. Snook and roosterfish bulge under the slack surface, though fishing is not allowed in the basin. We pick our way through the shoaled-up water, and Macklis points to a rusted dredge rig, silent and listing in the shallows.

Still, if you're looking for stern condemnation you won't hear it from Macklis. He likes the idea of a zipless run out the slot. That's where his heart lies, and the faster he can get there in his own panga—a 21-foot commercial sled he uses to handline *huachinango*—the better. There's also a touch of pride in seeing some modernity come to his lifelong home.

We run down the Mar to Punta Arena, its namesake sands turning the water all sorts of green. We manage a couple of small roosters, not much bigger than baguettes. But like every panga run I've ever taken, it's the overwhelming quiet and the focus of the hunt that nourishes. The fish always come. You earn the memorable hits with soul-crushing misses. It's never just a boat ride. You catalog and learn, running mental game tapes from past efforts. There's Cerro Colorado. Here's Las Barracas, where my father and I doubled down on striped marlin and heavy-shouldered bull dorado, our best day of fishing together. You see what the current is doing and what that means to the day's prospects.

Alonso is displaying *panguero* wisdom, turning so I can watch him carefully bridle a bait. He runs the needle through the eye sockets, ending with a sanitary double-loop of thread. It looks cleaner than a trussed quail in some Michelin-starred bistro. We continue on, telling him not to worry, that we fish plenty. We're here to have him show us his town, his waters. To make a few photographs. He nods and points the *Mosca Magic* back to the barn.

Later, when he's done cleaning fish with his *socios* under the trees, he joins us at the splendid Leonero bar. A light onshore breeze has set the palm fronds clacking. The window shutters are thrown open and the view, as always, is worth the price of a room. We make plans to meet at sunset at his house in town. His wife will show us some pictures, he says as he walks off. We're joined by Gary Barnes-Webb, the longtime manager of the Ranch. He runs an exceedingly tight ship and has the bearing of a fellow who could do what he does anywhere you drop him. Gary pops a beer and gives us a demonstration of Xhosa, the clicking language of his native South Africa's Zulu tribe. He does it deadpan, as if this is a perfectly natural thing to hear in Baja Sur.

I ask him what he thought about the rash of motor thefts.

"Listen," he says. "Do you know how the Somali pirates got started? The Japanese were running huge factory ships off the coast there, wiping out the Somalis' only means of survival. So they armed themselves, launched pangas, went far offshore to these towering vessels, scaled their sides, and just took the fecking things. That's how they got started. It was a life-or-death, defensive measure. They could use some balls like that around here." Gary exhibits that get-shit-done attitude I've seen in every South African expat I've met.

At Macklis' house, he comes out to greet us. First he gives us a full walkaround of his personal panga. Unlike his Rancho sled, this blue, bare-bones unit is custom-fitted for his personal needs. He crawls aboard and marches us through his quiver of winding boards. They're fat with shark mono and interchangeable leaders. He drops a weighted line over the rail. It lands with a puff of dust. "Too shallow!" he says. Mrs. Macklis comes out to the patio with several framed photos and an album. They page us through it all, pointing out epic catches and monster snapper hauls. She's amused by our presence and clearly proud of her man.

Macklis is back on his trailered skiff, coiling line into a bucket. He seems to have shifted gears, and it's time for us to leave. Backing out of the drive we have a clear view of the whole tableau: the jungle of a yard, the neat vegetable garden, the jigs hanging from a small guava tree. Tonight Macklis will be back on the anchor under the moon, hand-over-handing something up from the deep. Part Scot, part Mexican, and all *panguero*, he's a living picture of a *vagabundo* at rest and at home.

The Setenta-Mineral

From *The Surfer's Journal*, Volume 29, Number 1, 2020

•

Are you a waistline-conscious basic with the audacity to call a vodka soda a proper highball? If so, we'd rather you skip this and thus never be saved.

If you live on the mayonnaise side of the border, you'll be forgiven for not knowing that Don Julio 70 is Mexico's fastest-growing "call" tequila. You've been snowed by the brutally effective marketing of "ultra-premium" brands like Patrón, or that celebrity stuff jobbed out by an actor, a disco owner, and a developer with the deathlessly jejune, white-boys-in-Cabo nameplate that means "House of Friends." (A brand aimed directly at hedge-fund ferrets, preordained for a billion-dollar acquisition.)

This *gabacho* learned of 70 years ago while licking his wounds at his local—the Dandy del Sur—subsequent to a 2,000-peso beatdown at the hound track. Admittedly, big-house *cristalinos* lack the character of a fine small-batch *blanco*. But Julio is the true gen. It's a faultless *añejo cristalino*, even though it hails from a conglomerate (Cuervo). It's religiously distilled, aged for a year and a half in white oak, and then siphoned into 750mL bottles of 100-percent, hangover-free Jalisco throat wash. That's the magic of *cristalino* distillation.

That's providing you don't add sugars. Which you won't. Because no Mexican man will knowingly drink a margarita. Fact. (They will, however, kill tonnage of *palomas*, especially at weddings.) So top that 70 with *agua mineral*, preferably the source-bottled Agua de Piedra brand from Nuevo León. Garnish with a squeeze.

Not a Persian lime, for Chrissakes, a Mexican lime.

When you turn your friends on, we only ask that you tell 'em where you got it. Vodka soda fops are tone-deaf to attribution, but we agave cats always pay homage.

Our Man in the Antilles

Chris Klopf shoots the Dominican Republic.

From *The Surfer's Journal*, Volume 30, Issue 5, 2021

•

"Pezman says this portfolio feature is your gold watch."

Some 25 years ago, *TSJ* dispatched writer Steve Barilotti to Northern California to interview photographer Chris Klopf. Klopf was grateful for the attention, but unprepared for the tongue-in-cheek message the publisher had asked Barilotti to convey.

Klopf—46 at the time and decades into the game—was perplexed. What the hell was this? Some *pronunciamento*? Time to hang up the lenses and hit the porch? Under whose authority?

It's a velvet Caribbean evening in January 2021 and the night breeze is whatever degree of perfection you might prefer. We're at the kitchen table, windows thrown open, at Klopf's Dominican Republic winter *pensione*. He's riding out the curfew with takeaway plantain-topped sushi, reprising his "gold watch" reaction with a head tilt and an eye roll.

"I've always been freelance. I never shot for a magazine in my life," he says. He means it by way of explaining his lack of fealty to any publication.

That response bears the freight of his avocation. Veteran surf photographers are historically a wary and prickly lot. They've dealt with a Jungian soup of competitors, feckless pros, uncommunicative editors, late-arriving checks, and the clacking, flood-prone tools of their trade. One must forgive the masters of the form for their occasional harrumphs. I've learned to be reserved and earnest, as with dealing with South American immigration agents. It's best to feign a certain deference and have some baksheesh lipping out of your breast pocket.

Setting down my rum rickey on a paper towel, I look at Klopf and explain that "gold watch" undoubtedly meant a summation of his career to date. A chance to explain himself, photographically speaking, to the world at large. A reprise of his finest work. He chews on that, nodding his acceptance.

"Bro," he says. "You have to know I'm a rural guy. Back home, I live on a mountaintop in the redwoods. My closest neighbor is a Buddhist monastery, okay? I don't do well with hidden meanings."

Cool, I tell him. My own late-onset maturity has me, too, favoring the blunt. *Sin rodeo*, as they say.

That out of the way, we are free to talk beginnings.

"I started taking surf photos in 1965," Klopf says. "NorCal, Santa Barbara, Baja. Art Brewer [at *Surfer*] gave me 40 rolls of film in 1978 to go to Puerto Escondido with Vince Collier and Richard Schmidt. I nailed it that trip, and I came back, gave them all the photos, and they went, 'Um, these photos look too much like Pipeline, and we're not using them.' And I went, 'Huh, really?' I sent a few to *Surfing* mag and got a couple full pages or whatever. And shit, the rest popped out in my book frickin' 50 years after the fact."

I was aware of Klopf's work, both then and now. A lot of us are. Tantalizing reef morsels from the Sonoma coast ("Ten Spots You'll Probably Never Surf"). Black-and-white point lineups from Baja's sage-to-cirio transition zone. The aforementioned Puerto. Kirra-Indo-North Shore.

But it's his modern work that's seen him become a steady presence on the Tour de Groovy. Multiple runs to Northern Peru.

Long-form residencies in Costa Rica. Duty slogs in El Salvador and Nicaragua. All in the company of style hessians like Alex Knost, Tommy Witt, Jared Mell, Tyler Warren, Robin Kegel, and Justin Quintal. The new century rejuvenated Klopf creatively, if not practically. He's been traveling the world making surf photos for 40-odd years, and he's never bothered to shoot cats he wouldn't otherwise shoot. A human centipede of tripods on the beach for a surf contest? Pass.

But it's the place we are sitting that piqued me. While based in Mendocino, Klopf has traveled relentlessly, bunking down in Australia, Bali, the Philippines, Hawaii, and Costa Rica. Yet he's spent the last seven winters in the Dominican Republic. Does he know something we don't?

In short, yes. Sure, well-traveled East Coasters already know that adjacent Puerto Rico cops more swell, but the appeal of the DR to competent (versus elite) surfers is real. Affordable, spot-rich, Caribbean blue, a touch overlooked…just the sort of thing to lift them—and a stuffed-passport journeyman photographer—to at least half-mast. But if you're looking for Klopf to pin drop—to hand over the keys—you're exercising the sort of newb mores that he abhors. It's not simple drawbridge-expat shit. Those who have earned their way into the game know that it's not theirs to give. For that reason alone, Klopf says, the Dominican surfers retain all spot copyright.

"Let me be clear about that right now," he says.

Where his immigration here is concerned, it was a process of elimination.

"Well, I thought about the Philippines. I was on the island of Leyte in 1990, where Douglas MacArthur landed. I met a Filipina and I ended up falling in love with her, but I had to fly back to

Australia to edit footage. When I was done, I flew back and found her. It was before the internet, before any of that shit, and when I pulled up on a little frickin' tricycle, she was shocked: 'I never thought I'd see you again.' The mayor married us and I gave her dad, like, 100 bucks to go buy beer and stuff for everyone. We've been married ever since. I bought her a little restaurant near Mendocino. But to live in the Philippines? No. Too damn hot and too damn dangerous. Your life is worth 10 bucks. I know. I've been there at least 10 times."

Post-PI, Klopf worked his NorCal acreage, surfed his home breaks, and decamped to the Southern Hemisphere during the rain and cold of the northern winters. Driven and willfully recalcitrant, he's always taken pride in the old-school photographic disciplines. Follow focus. Continuous tone. Stopping down Fuji Velvia, then pushing the film past spec in processing for that gum-numbing late '80s color. It wasn't until deep into the aughts that he even tried digital.

Californian (now Bali-based) surfer Jared Mell remembers, "My first trip with Klopf was when I was 18. Costa Rica. We were hanging out after a good day and he gave me that Cheshire grin, holding up a Ziploc bag of exposed film, and said, 'Fuckkk, grom, we did it.'"

Justin Quintal is more effusive regarding Klopf's craft.

"I think there's something different that Klopf does," says Quintal. "A little more old school, probably from shooting film for so many years. It's rare you see him hold the button down on his camera. He once told me, 'It's not a machine gun.' I feel like he takes images with intention, and you see that in his work. I think his images stand out, and over the years he's retained a certain feel and a common thread."

As he tracked around the Pacific with his measured sniper's finger clocking Kentucky windage—Peru, Lombok, Queensland—he wasn't officially looking for a winter nest. But he wasn't *not* looking either. He almost found it in the most unsurprising location one might conjure.

"Yes, I ended up with a place in Costa Rica," he recalls. "It worked. Like I said, I'm a long-term guy. I'm not a 'surgical mission' guy. Today, CR is played out. It's like a global contingent of every nationality lives there and owns all the businesses. And the locals are the ones that work for [them]. And the money to fund the businesses comes from all, you know—they're South American or European or American or Canadian or whatever.

"And as a guy that likes to swim and shoot from the water, the crocs [are a pain]. Nowadays every river is filled with crocs, from Tamarindo to Ollie's. Every goddamned river.

"And if you leave anything in your car, it's going to be gone in Costa Rica. Instant smashed window. If you're in a parking lot of a ritzy hotel, your shit's gone. It doesn't matter if there's a security guard. So yeah, Costa Rica's done, man."

"What, Mexico? The places that I like don't have enough infrastructure," he says. "You end up living in the dirt. Nicaragua? El Salvador? Same deal as the Philippines: too hot, too dangerous."

Finishing dinner, he lays out a plan to give me a survey of the Dominican coast, a soup-to-nuts rundown that he says will voice his love for the DR in ways words can't. Over the next couple of weeks, we do just that.

The North Coast—centered around the town of Cabarete—is a complex of sand banks, coves, and reefs. Each of them glows and wanes under an ever-changing set of conditions. One can be faced with onshore doggerel at Reef A and, 300 yards away and unseen, Reef B is coming alive. Local knowledge is absolutely required. That's where the boys come in.

"The main surf spot—which I will mention because it's on Surfline [with a wave cam]—is Encuentro," says Klopf. "There's a surf camp, and the surf guides hang out there. Encuentro has about four or five peaks that have different moods. So all you do is look around and ask around, like Jorge Mijares or Chepe Gomez or Bobo Peralta or Brandon Sanford or Pedro Fernandez. Those are names to remember. If you see a guy surfing good, ask him, 'Dude, can you help me?' He'll point you in the right direction. Or he'll become your personal guide. If you think you're going to fly in and wing it and backpack it around the island and find all these waves, you're not going to find a goddamn thing. Because they're all hidden. There's so many little directions and nooks and crannies, and so many swell angles at different spots that are close to each other. There will be five different spots and they all break on different swell angles. Or different winds, you know?"

Driving the point home, we roll up to a guard kiosk fronting a gated community. The guard sees Klopf, offers an unsmiling thumbs-up, and waves us through.

"No way random Billy from Daytona Beach is getting in," Klopf says.

Finding a hole through the jungle to a hidden two-track, we bump past equestrians and shotgun-toting security. After a few minutes, the trail ends. Blinding white sand. The sort of blue water that has you questioning any allegiance you might have to tropical Pacific waypoints. A handful of beach creatures are lazing in the morning sun. Out on the reef, a three-wave set stands up, finds its footing, and offers itself up to the scant handful of surfers who chase one another into the bay. To the inexperienced

Caribbean visitor grasping for comparisons, it feels like Kauai in, oh, 1978. On an extraordinarily glassy day.

"The trades, bro," he says, reading the vibe. "So it's basically a southeast-angled wind. You don't usually get pure souths, but they have them from time to time. The south-angled wind is offshore on the North Coast. It's usually a morning wind."

Klopf can't help himself and double-taps a pair of handheld photographs. It's cloudless, but the weather is splitting the difference between cool and warm: 74-degree air, 80-degree water.

"I didn't come here trying to find anything," Klopf says. "I was trying to escape the winter, and the temperature was perfect, and I had some bros down here and then got introduced to a lot of the local surfers and I became friends with them. And, I don't know, I was mostly shooting lineups because no one believed there were waves here. And the spots, up to pretty much a year ago, were almost completely empty except Encuentro, which has a European influx of beginners and kiters.

"The affordability aspect is a factor, of course. In Costa Rica, a 5-gallon jug of good water can be 10 bucks. It's a dollar here. You could live here on $1,000 US, no problem. Once you figure it out and make some contacts, you could find an okay place for $400 a month.

"Food-wise, it's the typical home-kitchen *casado* style you'd find in Costa Rica: rice, beans, plantains, a little chunk of some protein. But everything's cheaper. Everything. If you want to eat cheap, you can. Fresh dorado, fresh mero. And you know what? You're probably getting fresher chicken than you would be if you were walking into a fancier restaurant. Because they're just taking one out in the back and fuckin' snappin' its neck and throwing it on the grill for ya.

"The people are chill. Maybe a little indifferent. They have to be chill because the tourist police are pretty heavy here. But there are ghetto-type areas farther away where some of the Dominican locals are pretty fuckin' rough. I mean, you can go right across the fence there to the rivermouth and you don't want to show up there without a local boy, 'cause it's [crime-ridden]. You might get poked.

"This is a country on a level with the Philippines as far as how much people are getting paid, and the Haitian workers work for even less. I want to see the local guys get the opportunities. Guiding, small surf shops. Rentals and surf lessons pay them pretty good, you know, but they need an influx of people. Encuentro is the spot. It has the soft, easy, hair-dry paddle out, and it's also got a shallow, urchin-studded Latin reef where you can get barreled."

There's something comforting about seeing a pirate at rest. At 70-something, Klopf has found his Goldilocks "just right" bed. Midway through the assignment, we trip down to a local novelty wave. Klopf has fired maybe a million frames of other guys surfing in the DR, but a severe neck injury has kept him off the wax for nearly a decade. I watch him paddle into a backwash-troubled right, stick the drop, and run down the line. I expect him to coast in on this small, remarkable victory. He executes a whippy kickout and commences to paddle back up the point.

Reefed

An unsung Baja harbor offers quick access for a land-based hit to Sacramento Reef.

From *The Bight*, Volume 1, Number 2, 2017

•

SS Sacramento, At Sea
December 5, 1872
To: CF Taggart
Agent, PMSS Co, San Diego

The steamship Sacramento *went on shore 190 miles to the southward and eastward of San Diego. Weather quiet. If there is a steamer in port please send her to our assistance. Everybody safe. Will remain on board until I hear from you.*

Yours respectfully,
EL Farnsworth

PS: The ship is filled with water and lays quiet on the reef.

Despite the obvious piloting error, you have to hoist your glass to Farnsworth. Ship busted-up on the rocks miles from a foreign shore. The nearest land a barren, wave-pounded island upswell, upwind, and upcurrent. No Coast Guard. No radio. But check that message. Like he's asking a neighbor for a cup of flour. He had to have known the conditions were sure to change, that the grease calm would unravel, turning "the Reef" into a total goat rope. The fates smiled, the passengers were rowed to safety, and the message boat got the news to the north. A happy ending. That record would not stand.

Shoals are generally discovered by their victims. The barely submerged rock complex was an anonymous smear on the horizon until it was surveyed by the *USS Hassler* following the wreck of the *Sacramento*. But a name on a chart is no guarantee of safe passage. In 1969, millionaire industrialist Ralph Larrabee stacked into the Reef on his racing schooner, *Goodwill*. Nine perished, no survivors. The shoal will always be a hazard and, for about the same reason that I avoid discount sashimi, modern mariners give it a wide berth.

Fishermen, of course, seek it out. And fishing aside, it's not without appeal. Lying four miles hard to the south of Isla San Jerónimo, the Reef isn't much different from the peninsula to the east. Both the land and the Reef hide their charms.

Punta San Antonio, the closest continental presence, lies at a transitional latitude. The dry coastal scrub of the north begins to give way to the charismatic flora of the Valle de los Cirios. Crazed boojums grow like the smoke plumes of out-of-control rockets. Fat barrel cactus, rain-plump and purple, squat like dwarves. Cardons, the tallest cacti on earth, make their first appearance. The mountains inland are home to coyote, deer, lion, and *borrego*. Like the fish of the Reef, the animals are hidden by geography and seldom seen. And, as with the inland sierra, the Reef is full of life. Yellows, lobster, sea bass, whitefish, double-digit calico—it's here in the sort of abundance that strains credulity.

It's not like it hasn't been fished. It's 2015, for God's sake. More than seven-billion meat puppets tread the globe, hunting for protein and looking for kicks. Occasionally, charter pangas make the 50-mile sleigh ride from San Quintín. San Diego sportboats enact the odd stop, sometimes laden with skiffs and kayaks. And until the spring of 2014, there was no efficient way to day-fish the place.

We'd gotten wind of a new harbor punched in at Punta San Antonio. I was told it wasn't a particularly welcoming place for fishermen from the north, and focused purely on lobster and a couple of short finfish seasons. Trailer boats weren't allowed to use the new concrete ramp, and even if there was an open invite, the road in would bounce your rig to scrap.

But doesn't all of that fairly beg for a proof-of-concept run? A dirt-road barnstorm with no promise of success? It would come down to finding a *panguero*. Like elsewhere on the peninsula, if you're willing to take potluck on a boat with no bait tank, no electronics, but plenty of local knowledge, the commercial boys can get you sorted—and usually on the cheap.

The Sacramento Reef resource belongs to the *pescadores* of Punta San Antonio. As with fishing *ejidos* up and down the Baja coast, the PSA co-op works under quotas, boat and motor subsidies, and bears the responsibility for beating back poachers and competing fishermen. How they convinced the government to carve a high-cost harbor is anyone's guess. Where environmental impact is concerned, the desolate location surely played a role. The point lies precisely at the junction of East Jesus and BFE, and is hardly an attraction for the average traveler. It's cold, windy, and flyblown, lacking the wetlands and whales that serve as rallying flags for conservation efforts farther south. Yet regardless of how it came to be, there it is—the only floating-dock slipped marina between Ensenada and Cabo San Lucas. Until now, it's gone unrecorded in any fishing media.

Our guidelines for the strike mission were strict. Seventy-two hours. Set dates. Rain or shine. No contacts. No reservations. Two trucks. Fifth-grade Spanish. Micro-budget. The stated goal? At least one day of fishing at what some call—not without merit—"Calico National Park." The unstated goal: Don't end up T-boning the reef like Captain Farnsworth.

During a typically effortless six-hour glide down Mexico 1, our small crew got acquainted. Hayward and me are all too familiar with one another. The addition of confirmed bass freaks Justin Reynolds and Randy Spizer helped chew up the miles. Reynolds orchestrates a superb little blog, Radio Silence Fishing, and is endlessly creative behind the lens. His buddy Spizer is a veteran of countless skiff runs to San Clemente Island with Reynolds, where they're devotees of the foam, all but rail-clacking off the rocks in the boiler zone. It looks kind of heavy and violates all sorts of common sense, but that's where the bigger-grade calicos hang. They were looking forward to running their program at the Reef.

Rolling into El Rosario, the Semana Santa travelers had the dusty onion-growing town hanging "No Vacancy" signs. We played a hole card, driving to the outskirts to the optimistically named Baja's Best motel. As we quickly found, it sure as hell wasn't the worst. Run by ex-commercial cat Ed Luske, it's a pleasant compound secured behind a rolling gate. Our room had four huge beds and private parking—no need to load and unload. I shanghaied a motel employee and told him our plan. He promptly jumped in the truck, guiding me to Abajo, a small village a couple of miles west. He pointed out a house and said to be there at five o'clock the following morning. A "Ricardo" would be happy to help us out.

Back at the Best, we were the sole clients for dinner. We asked for a menu and were told, "The menu is chile rellenos stuffed with local crab. Would you like a drink?" The waitress walked away, returning with four goblets of ice. She topped them off with a better-than-average *reposado*. Right out of central casting, a herd of chihuahuas scurried around our feet. Maybe some sheephead ate fresher crab than we did that night, but that can't be proved.

Dawn found us banging down the coast, alternating between graded velvet and chopped-up two-track. The 4WD switch was never even glanced at. Ricardo rode between the bass freaks, his 20-gallon drum of gas tied down in the truck bed. Dropping down into the harbor, he pointed out to the Reef and said it could go either way. Even at dawn there was a light northerly beginning to freshen.

The harbor is incongruous in the extreme. Essentially, it's a crater in the ground, with a slim channel cutting through the cliffs to the open ocean. There's a modern, designer-looking bath house and cleaning station with a roof deck to check the conditions out at the Reef, visible on the horizon. A steep but well-placed ramp and four British-built iron hoists mark the edges, and a couple dozen slips give it a finished look. Down at the panga, Ricardo stopped me. He asked in Spanish, "Do you have slicks? Do you have PFDs?" "No," I said. He stared down at his feet for a couple of beats, looked back up at me, and asked, "Why not?"

Fair question. Running out to Sacramento in all but birdbath-calm days demands basic safety measures. After some rummaging, he found four kits of gear in a dock box and we got ourselves zipped in for the run out the entrada.

With about 4 feet of west swell and plenty of tide, timing the channel was straightforward. Much more, though, and the dogleg jetty could get your attention in a "roll the boat and mulch you into chorizo on the barnacled cliff face" kind of way. Given the slop and our heavily laden craft, the crossing took about 20 minutes. There was so much whale in the water that it was comical. Dozens of the beasts were heading north from Ojo de Liebre, Mag Bay, and San Carlos. They were in no hurry, performing the cetacean *Kama Sutra* everywhere we looked. At one point, a ménage of them sounded eight feet off the bow. We all but skidded into the boil.

Nearing the Reef, the importance of a dialed pilot was obvious. Swells came from all compass points: peaks, horseshoes, pop-up widow makers. And this was a mildly sloppy day. The water had rolled, dropping a good four points that week. For this zone, April is about the worst month you can choose. This wasn't going to be any sort of wide-open fiesta. Ricardo set us on a drift on the outside corner of some kelp. Extra-large swimbaits and the odd surface iron were deployed. Reynolds and Spizer started running the diagnostics, island-honed experience informing their attack. Hayward, nothing if not a traditionalist, chucked the plug, with a long sink-out leading to the first checkerboard of the day. In between the wave dodging we began a steady, if lackluster, pick. The grade, however, couldn't be argued with and spoke to the possibilities during better conditions. Four-pound calico were common, with a couple of bigger editions getting bounced.

Spizer, a former X Games inline skater, I kid you not, lived on the bow, doing a 300-beats-per-minute techno shuffle to avoid getting pitched. That's how they play it up in the land of the electric trolling motor. Ricardo was quietly chuckling, waiting for the inevitable, when Spizer landed a muscled-up six pounder.

By noon, the wind had us turning tail. We weren't halfway back before planning a future visit. As is so often the case, the escape and sense of surprise made the peninsula resonate. At the gas stations, on the dirt roads, at the harbor, on the Reef—we didn't see Gringo One. Back at the motel, Luske asked us how it went. We filled him in, asking about the new harbor. He explained that he runs charters out of nearby Punta Baja. Their co-op isn't allowed access to the Reef, instead fishing the equally superb waters of Isla San Jerónimo. The PSA boys have the Reef on lock. He went on to describe how he hosted a wedding that included families from both camps. The Punta Baja clan are *religiosos*, shunning booze. The San Antonio gang rolled in with hundreds of pounds of ice and about three million cans of beer. The affair ended predictably, with the fishermen duking it out in the onion field out back. Just as predictably, all was forgotten come morning. Luske knows the territory and has probably forgotten more about fishing the El Roso zone than most will ever know—excepting the *pangueros*.

The wind came up, and we opted to head north to San Quintín for a night's rest and a meal at the Mill. Like Farnsworth, we'd gotten an eyeful. By day three, we were home and calling this exploratory run a worthy use of a long weekend.

Stackin' 'Em

Kelly Catian y Familia de San Quintín.

As told to Scott Hulet

•

There are two categories of fishermen in Southern California: Those who have fished San Quintín, and those who are curious about it. A reasonable five-hour drive south of the border, San Q holds the sort of appeal that Ensenada had in the '50s. Ensenada—once heralded as the "Yellowtail Capital of the World" by local boosters and outdoor writers—finds itself greatly diminished in modern times due to overharvesting of both sardine fin bait and the creatures who feed on them. As such, San Quintín is currently considered the closest Mexican Pacific fishing destination with hotels, charter services, and a relatively robust fishery.

While originally known for steady groundfishing for rock cod and lings, a confluence of events has led to the humble agricultural town earning a name as a choice place to lock into trophy-class yellows and white sea bass. The high spots a short run from the mouth of the bay, and the coastal kelp beds found along the Socorro-Arroyo Hondo stretch to the south, have become highly regarded hunting grounds for fat croaker and rod-flexing jacks. And while a day trip for similar species in a well-founded pilothouse or other big skiff on the US side runs well over $1,000 a day, San Quintín offers a similar shot for about half of that.

With spartan but inexpensive lodging and good grub easily available, it's not hard to graph San Q's appeal. As recently as the early '80s, there was a scant handful of Yamaha Enduro-powered bench-seat pangas servicing the trade. Today, options have grown considerably, from the bare-bones rigs of yore on up to fully rigged Parkers with huge live-bait capacity and a rack of electronics. You can find capable pangueros *on both ends of the spectrum, but if you're looking for the local highliner, one must at least put veteran captain Kelly Catian on the list.*

Part of that is sheer visibility. With a trio of Parkers and a custom super panga—expertly run by Kelly and his sons Oscar, 30, George, 27, and ace fish cutter, Christian, 26—K&M is an obvious daily presence at the Old Mill launch ramp. Beyond that, Kelly was the first local operator to have a polished online presence, bridging the gap between deep local knowledge and tech'd-up charter marketing.

With general watermanship gleaned from a life of spearfishing, surfing, and commercial work, Kelly's knowledge of the often sketchy local waters makes him something of a go-to. Indeed, when SoCal charter captains drop down for a busman's holiday, they're generally found on a K&M boat. Some are lucky enough to visit the Catian family compound for a homemade meal, moments from the Old Mill, with its view of the back bay and the extinct volcanoes that dominate the coastal view plane. Kelly, 50, lords over this salty redoubt with his lovely local wife, Bertha Alicia.

This background roll-in isn't meant to butter Kelly's muffin. To the contrary. We need him more than he needs the business—we wanted to find a trusted local voice to lay down the underpinnings of the San Q program for Bight *readers. Obviously, the best way to do that was to spend a few trips getting to know Kelly, his family, and his waters. Here's his take on San Q, both its fishing history and its current situation.*

From what I understand, it all began with Geni Schafer in the 1960s. It was called the Old Mill Boat House and was later sold to Alfonso and Dorothy Vela. They had it forever, until Al Gaston got it around '89. He made it what it was—it was nothing when he got it, and he reigned until 2008 or '09 when there was a weird, hostile takeover. He got it swindled out from underneath him by a guy named La Rosa, who then got swindled out by a local dude named Carlos Hoffin, who was from some huge Mormon family. Supposedly he had something like 50 brothers and sisters. He was a Mexican dude but I think he might have been born in the States. He spoke really good English and was talkative. He ran it into the ground, at which point he was approached by Los Pinos [the tomato barons of the Valle de San Quintín]. They've run it since.

My dad started fishing here in the late '70s—all over Mexico, in fact. I was born in Lynnwood, California, and went to elementary school in West Covina. My parents—Filipino dad, French mom—split when I was 17. They were both school teachers and my dad was also a radiologist, and he just came home one day and said, "Yeah, we've figured out where we are going to move and retire—and we're outta here." I was like, "Really? What about me?" And they said, "We'll give you a few hundred bucks, and good luck." I took over his job. He said, "Don't hire your stupid friends." And of course I hired my stupid friends, bombed that place within a year, lost all these big contracts. He had done non-destructive testing for aircraft companies and he had a shop in LA. A year later he asked me how things were going, and I said, "We pretty much blew it." I thought he was going to be super pissed but he said, "Why don't you come down here."

I didn't really know where "here" was. I remember at that time I didn't realize that Baja was in Mexico. I thought San Quintín was near Lake Elsinore or something. They told me to come down and hang out, stay for a couple of weeks, "and get your shit together and we'll give you a couple of bucks and go back and hit it again" or whatever. That was around 1985. I surfed but wasn't super into fishing. We had chased albacore back in the States and did a million trips where we trolled for 24 hours and never caught anything—so my whole thing for fishing was, like, nah. The first time I went fishing here, we stacked white sea bass inside the bay from an anchored boat, literally stacked all day, and from then on

I was totally into it. Dad had a boat and captain, and made it clear that I couldn't just come in and take this dude's job. I had got to learn the ropes. My dad said, "When this dude is done then you can run the boat, but in the meantime you deck for him."

Pedro's Pangas, Garcia's, that had all kind of started after the Old Mill showed up. When Pedro got here he blew the fishing up—he went out and got some real boats. But even at that point, there wasn't a bunch of real skippers. He was pulling waiters out of the restaurant, you know what I mean? The guys running boats now weren't fishermen at first. Jaimie was a waiter at the Old Mill, he got pulled in as an emergency. Lilo, those guys were from the Bay of LA. He wasn't super accepted—everyone was kind of standoffish or whatever—but he has put his time in.

Juan Cook was born here. He left and went to the States when he was around 18, lived there until he was way older. He would come back sporadically. He fished with [highly regarded San Diego captain] John Grabowski a lot, fished on the *Qualifier 105* as a passenger, and he learned a lot about fishing. I think he was up in Alaska too. I remember him calling me when I first started K&M. He had decided to come back here because he heard that it was starting to happen and that there was sportfishing and this and that. Everyone knew he was a good skipper. The whole scene has really taken off over the last 10 years or so.

When I was fishing with my dad, the heavy guys included Tiburon and the Duartes, who I learned from. The Duartes were commercial fishermen and hunters. They were the first and probably some of the best sportfishing guides. They are still doing it, just on a private, semi-retired level. They're still really into the hunting. Don Gato, the oldest fisherman in all of San Q, was the first guy. My dad fished with him. He's still here at Gatos Palapas.

When I first got here he was kind of our doorway, and pretty much the reason my dad moved here. Then I got taught by all these other guys. I guess that's why they respected me a little bit more, because I wasn't just some gringo kid that came in saying, "Hey, you're off the boat." He pretty much had to walk off that boat before I got to touch it. They thought that was cool.

My mom introduced me to my wife. I was just here for a couple weeks, planning to make some cash and go back to the States, you know? My mom was like, "You have to meet this girl" and I'm like, "Nah, I don't want to meet no girls." But I met her and ended up staying here and never went back, and that's pretty much it.

I ended up being the first guy to have a fish finder. First one to have a bait tank. I used to go and put everyone on fish. I set up the first rock cod market out of here. The buyer would call me with an order and I would get however many pangas to go out, I'd use the fish finder, and be like "Hey, drop 'em here." This was with hand lines and buoys, no one had rods and reels. We used bazookas, a PVC tube about six feet long. You cut a slit from stem to stern on it to hold whole baited rigs. See, when you have a 150-hook longline, to launch that thing off a boat you would have to bait each hook individually and start draping the line over the gunwales. But the problem with 150-foot longline is it is going to take 10 minutes to launch that thing off the boat and down, and when you are metering and there is current and it is super deep your chances of hitting are zero. So the bazooka was an old commercial method of getting those things down quick.

The fishery down here has definitely changed. The rockfish doesn't compare to how it used to be, but other things are better. When I started fishing you never saw guys catch 15 yellowtail in a day. If you caught two you were lucky. Back then there wasn't braid. All there was was mono. The reels were clunkier.

I remember seeing big sportboats killing it out there. That was when I told myself, "You *have* to get a bait tank." I think for a couple of years when I first started using bait no one really followed suit. The panga guys were like, "Screw having a battery on the boat," but we were killing it then. If you dropped a live mac anywhere near the 240—if you wanted to put 20 on the boat, you could easily. Soon everybody figured it out. They got bait tanks and soon after everyone was slaying, you know what I mean?

When I first moved here no one went for tuna, ever. It was rock cod and bottom fish. Occasionally, yellowtail or sea bass. It has transitioned from a groundfish place to a sportfish place. Probably mostly due to the boats and the gear, the experience of the skippers, and stuff like that. The commercial fleet just keeps on growing. A lot of guys do sport and commercial. The guys that I learned from went all commercial. They really don't like the stress of dealing with people. At one point I remember them being burnt on the whole tourism thing. When I first got here fish wasn't worth as much money as it is now.

There is no government funding for tourism. I don't know why. But if you have a commercial permit you can get new engines, whatever you want. They don't pay for anything. And especially now that Mexico is in a bind and getting shut down by the US. I just went to a government meeting and they have programs for everything. New engines. Diesel trucks. Stuff for big operations. They're kicking down. But they don't want to give it to the tourist sector for some reason. And the sad thing is we are not allowed to have two licenses on one boat. So if I have a sportfishing license I can't have a commercial. If I want to commercial fish I have to have a separate boat, which is kind of retarded. We try to explain to these guys that most fishermen only own one boat and they can't make it on sportfishing alone. Fish and game are just as backward down here as they are up there.

Most of the local commercial fishermen were born here. They don't tolerate outsiders. The geoduck clam gold rush changed that for good. The arrival of the bait boat fleet [for the tuna pens in Ensenada] and other threats to the resource really made everyone open their eyes. You aren't going to go anywhere around here—within 20 miles—and get a good commercial haul. It's not like it was. Most of those guys are going long, fishing down below Isla Jerónimo and stuff like that. There's fish around here, but it's been 30 years of hittin' it hard, at least as far as the bottomfish guys go.

I think the reason there weren't as many problems back in those days was because there was no market for yellowtail. You couldn't really sell it. It was a secondary fish, and you would get hardly anything for it. Now there is a market, and when the local commercial guys see a San Diego sportboat pull 300 fish in a day, well, it has sucked everyone back together again. The young guys are looking up fish-and-game laws on the internet. Everyone is a team now.

I think the actions of other people on the coast and the way they protect their fishery has finally had an impact on all these guys. Abreojos is full lockdown. They don't have issues with anyone trying to fish that area. Everyone just knows. The waiting list to get in on that co-op is huge. If you aren't family, it's not going to happen. El Rosario has one now too. They have their little patrol boat. We even have one now, believe it or not, a Skipjack called *Robo Cop*.

The engine down here that drives the place is the 240. That's everyone's bread-and-butter spot, and that's what we're most protective of. The younger generation of fishermen, the 30 year olds down here, they're smarter than any of us were. A lot of them went to college. Some of them are commercial fishing, but also have careers like dentistry, real jobs on the side. When I was growing up, the attitude was that the fishermen don't want any trouble. We would have a bump in with a sportboat every once in a while, but we never real issues. It's different now. More boats. The younger guys around here recognize it's their future.

There is a way where it could be done so everyone could fish. The sportboat guys, in the old days, you didn't have to tell them that. They would know. People down here don't want any kind of hassles. For years they would go out of their way and just let those boats go off to avoid any kind of hassle. They don't want to get into a yelling match out there. There came a point where I knew I was going to have to take a side. For years, a lot of skippers from San Diego knew me and would call me on their way down here and ask what's going on, and I would tell them. They would hook me up with bait. It wasn't an issue. They weren't trashing the place. Not that having a wide-open day is a bad thing, but there comes a point where you have to listen to the people that live there because they're barking at you—and that's the thing, it was just too easy to ignore people especially if there was like three sportboats out there. We'll see how it goes this year.

Café Racer

Miguel Tudela pins it through greater Lima's surf culture.

From *The Surfer's Journal*, Volume 32, Number 4, 2023

∙

Picture Peru. If you haven't had the pleasure, summon clichés. Employ prejudice.

Plump reed boats in the surf. An arid landscape of cinderblock low-rises and garish buses. Hangover-free, kitten-soft, ether-washed powder from the Ica Valley. Two-stroke moto taxis buzzing like wasps. That highland flute music the eat-pray-love backpackers lose their shit over. Improbably long left points with a backdrop of oil platforms and artisanal squid boats.

Yet none of these are in evidence in Punta Hermosa, the bustling-but-relaxed surf suburb an hour south of Lima. Isla Ballesta Street in June feels more like Lisbon than rural South America. European-style shops defy the dusty surroundings. Sport wagons and Rovers pass through gated *privada* checkpoints. It's a town clearly on some slow, deliberate come-up. This is the home of Charcutería Lucaffé, the storefront owned and operated by WSL and Olympic surfer Miguel Tudela and his fiancée, model-entrepreneur Alessandra Bonelli.

Bonelli discovered the Italian espresso brand on her travels, arranged a Peruvian license, and now imports Lucaffé, using the Charcutería as the mothership. Tudela's energy and local-hero status supercharged the launch. The deli is now a gathering point for townsfolk, surfers or not. A jersey and a cover shot or two adorn the interior, but it's undersold—not the sort of surf-kitsch overload you'd see in Redondo. Tudela pulls me a *cortado* as Bonelli glides across the street to pick up the daily pastry from the bakery. Sitting at a sidewalk table, we get beaned up and take the measure of the day.

It's gray. Peruvian winters are comically socked in, six months of overcast endured by the Limeños with stoic acceptance. If David Lynch spoke Spanish, he'd scout wintertime Peru for gloom appeal alone. It tests a visitor's mettle. Even a Californian inured to the Golden State's Catalina eddy. It's a mid-grade sort of misery, a vitamin D–depleting loss of one's own shadow.

A conspiracy of young surf rats scuttles around, issuing a stream of *puta*s. Every sentence in Peru includes this expletive. Locals use it like Mexicans use *verga* or Americans use "like," its literal meaning subordinate to enthusiasm. Depending on inflection, it can mean "Goddamn it," "Are you shitting me?" or "That's really cool." It's as harmless as it gets. Peruvians are notoriously gracious and polite. The "whore"-rapping rats respectfully calm down and grin as they pass our table.

Tudela charts our next few days. It includes a deep look at the points and reefs here in town—favored spot checks, paddle-out put-ins, angle shots, secret hideouts from ill winds. Punta Hermosa is a beneficially complex zone. Something for every approach, from rippable but imperfect reefs and beachbreak to shelf ledges to a foam-streaked granddaddy of a big wave.

When George Downing made his first visit to Lima, in 1955, he went up in a small plane to check the frontier. Mere minutes from the capital, he found Hermosa. It was unknown to the city surfers. Downing guided them in, and Gen 1 pioneers like Miguel Plaza and Piti Block had the privilege of naming rights and the pleasure of laying first tracks. Kon Tiki, Señoritas, Caballeros, Punta Rocas, and Playa Norte are the go-tos.

The Hawaiians had powerful influence here, even pre-Downing. Carlos Dogny Larco, an influential Limeño, discovered surfing on Oahu in the 1930s as a young man. He was tutored by no less than Duke and Rabbit. Inspired, Dogny returned to Peru to found Club Waikiki and advocate for further transpacific brotherhood. It's Peruvian surfing's New Testament, all on display at Club Waikiki and also at the Kon-Tiki Surfboards Museum in Punta Hermosa, lovingly owned and curated by august Peruvian surfer José Schiaffino.

Tudela knows the place well. He knocks on the door of the private oceanfront house where the Kon-Tiki museum is located. A distinguished fellow in his eighties lets us in, offering us a pisco. The walls and ceiling catalog some 70 years. Tudela points up to a Greg Noll Films full gun, walking through the relationship between the spears Noll built for Pico Alto and the Pomar brothers. Modern Peruvian surfers on the whole seem comparatively connected to their surf history. Tudela's no exception. He's lived his whole life at Hermosa, steeped in influence, and while he's a national sporting celebrity, people tend to respect his privacy. The town itself plays an obvious role in his success.

"It's one of the most consistent places in the world," he says. "We have big waves, points, long ones and short ones. Any wind direction. It's a great place to train."

By the 1970s, the town had become the home of Lima-area surfing. The waves of the nearby capital are, alas, bereft of any real quality. In season, the left point at Herradura stands alone as the only viable option. That's why Tudela's parents—both lifelong surfers—live in the south, hard against the rocky, kelp-riddled, temperate waters of Playa Hermosa.

The importance of the surfscape can't be overstated.

Like the best of the best—Slater, Florence, Ho—Tudela is a weapon from 1 to 30 feet. Tubes, airs, bombs: All are in his range of fluency, and all can be on offer right at the base of the bluff here in Hermosa.

His father, an early inhabitant of the town, paddled Miguel out to Pico Alto at the same age he first surfed it: 13. They made it a heritage session, a tribute. No wetsuits, no cords, no inflatable vests. Twenty feet, a mile out to sea. It left a mark, and Tudela considers Pico a part of his DNA. It also speaks to his fascination with large, serious, old-school venues like Waimea and Todos Santos, where sheer mass and terminal velocity connect him to those early go-outs with his father—and Peru's surfing patrimony.

Tudela's local crew refers to Pico Alto as "the Temple." Like many global big-wave venues, the place inspires reverence. The paddle-out itself can take half an hour. Often shrouded in fog, the glassy walls can go legit XXL, spooling off like a revved-up, cool-water Sunset Beach. First surfed by foundational Peruvian surfer Miguel Plaza and friends, the wave has played host to a catalog of big-wave freebooters, including Richard Schmidt, James Jones, and the late Mark Foo.

Tudela is obsessed with the place, and constantly looking for ways to elevate his performance. "I'm really working on finding the exact board to do what I want on the wave," he says. "I started building specific boards with [Al and Britt] Merrick, trying to find how small we can go and still paddle into them, but also turn like a shortboard. You want to get on those walls and just enjoy them, you know? Also, we've really studied rescue. We haven't had any rides recently that ended up in the hospital."

Surfing the less scale-rigorous World Qualifying Series for the WSL finds him on the road, with at least five international trips a year—Europe, Australia, the US, South Africa. It's enough of a gruel that he appreciates his hometown in ways that less geographically anchored surfers might not. Beyond that, there's plenty of competitive inspiration here and in the country at large.

"My inspiration was right here at home," Tudela says. "Yeah, my favorite surfers from abroad were Mick, Andy, and Kelly, but my guidance came from Gabriel Villarán, Cristobal De Col, Sofía Mulánovich, and Gabriel Aramburu. The guys coming up—Carlos Mario [Zapata], Lucca Mesinas, Alonso Correa, Joaquin Del Castillo—are pushing everyone super hard."

"But," he continues, "for me, Sofía is the biggest name in sport in Peru, and of course she changed everything. She made her dream come true—number one in the world. She inspired many, and also put surfing on the map for investors as a golden sport in Peru. We need to thank her for really making Peru be recognized as one of the best in surfing."

Loading up, we head to Miraflores, the cosmopolitan Lima district famed for its parks, rooftop bars, and outrageous criollo cuisine, the latter a perpetual eye-opener—like Spanish food if it went to *saucier* school in Lyon, grabbed a minor in Sinaloan shellfish, and finished with a Kanazawa sushi seminar. But it's sui generis, not assembled from parts. It's the top class of South American gastronomy, with no real second place, and an easily argued global top five. Breathe in the dense layers of a "simple" *arroz con mariscos*. You'll have to take a knee. It can be attributed only to *la brujería de los Andes*—the witchcraft of the high country, the place from which all blessings (and the yellow *ají* pepper) flow.

While the waves won't snap your flag to attention, Miraflores is one of the most unexpectedly surprising cities in the world. Consistent—and consistently blurpy—beachbreak lies at the foot of the low cliffs, shapeless and vaguely tourmaline-like. But it's a fertile city, worth far more attention than it gets from the average visitor, breaking in their boots on their way to the tourist-clogged gates of Machu Picchu. There's no closing time. Prowl the 3 a.m. side streets and listen, smell. Check the Martinez Tailor Shop, where you can get chalked up for a custom suit, find a hidden panel door, and tumble into a speakeasy crowded with Peruanas leaving lipstick on their Negronis. Soak up the revelry with a *chicharrón* sandwich and strawberry juice at La Lucha, one of the world's finest fast-food chains. It handily waxes Thomas Keller–approved In-N-Out with their fries alone. (You might know that every potato on the planet traces its rootstock to Peru, long before Ireland or Idaho.) Pursue some psychedelic *chicha*, that rolling, '60s-based Amazonian *cumbia* that still bumps if you have a clued-in fixer. Miraflores is the sort of place one could make a base of operations, darting up to Cabo Blanco or down to Cerro Azul when the charts flare…unless you're Tudela. He's on the discipline trip, with Olympic gold on his mind. The *cumbia* can wait.

Tudela is known among his young surfing associates as serious and driven. "He's basically done it all himself," his lifelong friend Jose Plaza told me. "He's always been that way. He had to. It's who he is. It's not like he came from money. And he's never been the type to just take what comes. He makes things happen."

Tudela is a fish who breathes—organized, high functioning, and well capable of crawling out of the shorebreak and onto the streets, résumé in hand, to find backing for his aspirations. Punta Hermosa isn't Coolangatta or Ventura or the North Shore, however. There's no phalanx of photographers stuffing memory cards with your every wave. That means the sole route to pro-dom is contest surfing, and the only real way to fund campaigns has been through international corporate backing. Trading on early competitive successes and reaching a zenith with his appearance at the 2020 Olympic Games, Tudela now has sponsors that include Volcom, Adidas, Monster Energy, Skullcandy, and Audi Peru. It's a heady little portfolio, and speaks to his willingness to knock on doors. His surfboard relationship is a case in point.

"When I made the decision to become a professional surfer," Tudela says, "the best guys in the world rode for Channel Islands. It was the era of Kelly. So I decided to start at the top. I've never left."

Last year, he was armed with 38 pieces of Britt Merrick matériel. A broad and deep batch, from 5'7" plugs to 10'2" guns for Pico Alto, Waimea, and his favorite Latin American wave, Chile's Punta de Lobos. Thirty-eight boards would seem bratty and excessive to some, but when one makes their bones at Pipeline, at Pico, and well above the lip everywhere else, they are more than some expense-able flex. They're daily bread.

The next morning, we meet in Miraflores at the hallowed Club Waikiki. It's a shadow-box display of golden-era Peruvian surf life, a midcentury-modern refuge for members only. In its heyday it was a blend of *Casino*-era Vegas and an Argentine polo club. Pisco sours on the deck, *très sportif* power brokers playing paddle tennis, board caddies, and brunette updos in bikinis. All still extant today. The populist leftists hated it, and when they fell into power in the '70s, they paved a thoroughfare right over the beachfront entrance as a double-fisted fuck you. Yet here the club stays, a testament to Carlos Dogny, the Hawaiian lifestyle he chose to emulate, and the country's connection to surfing itself.

Tudela is an honorary member and trains regularly at the club pool. He's treated with an easy deference, like a favored son. His trophies stand in a place of honor. The director arranges poolside plates of appetizers and drinks. After our meal, we drop downstairs to the locker room. It's a mind-bending catacomb of surfboards new and old. Favored tankers from the Peru International Surfing Championships era. Forgotten designs from the '70s, '80s, and '90s. Hundreds of daily drivers racked for modern members. All told, there are more than a thousand sleds, all curried and clucked over by the same boardmaster who looked after the personal spears of Noll, Cabell, and Pomar. Of course, Tudela keeps a short-stack quiver on hand. Out front, the waves provide a reasonable facsimile of the beachbreak hash often found in the contest milieu. Chiba, HB, Rio. Tudela looks at it like doing burpees between sets at the Corcoran iron pile. A way to get reps in the sun for future battles.

It's been paying off. In flashes of brilliance, like his buzzer-beating McTwist that heartlessly dispatched Griffin Colapinto in Brazil. In straight-up WQS wins, as he did in the Galápagos. In heavy-wave blitzes, like his semifinal run at the Volcom Pipe Pro. But the chance to represent his country in the 2020 Olympic Games brought him the level of national esteem normally reserved for soccer stars and F1 drivers. Like Mulánovich before him, he's become the face of Peruvian sport.

"It was a dream come true," says Tudela. "I think every athlete dreams of the Olympic Games. Tokyo was an amazing experience, and one of the proudest moments in my life."

At 28 years old, Tudela has achieved journeyman status. His goals for 2023 include climbing a few 'QS slots in the quest for WCT inclusion. Beyond that, he's focused on the Pan Am Games qualifiers for the 2024 Olympics and the possibility of competing for gold in Tahiti.

Sitting on the deck of his oceanfront house at Playa Norte, Pico Alto in the near distance, one can see the faint outline of his future. The Temple booms through the night. One hundred board feet of CI guns are stashed in the spare room. The café is moments away up the hill. Ratings and contests aside, it feels like a catbird seat. Away from the hue and cry of traditional US and Australian surf centers, Tudela inhabits a fully round surfer's life, living and working among friends, family, and the 90 or so surfers who call Punta Hermosa home.

There's an unofficial national anthem in the country called "Contigo Perú." It's played at soccer matches and is employed whenever Peruvians come together. When its lilting strains are first heard at events, everyone cheers and sings along. Not a dry eye in the house.

> *Binding the coast*
> *Binding the mountain range*
> *Binding the jungle*
> *With you, Peru*
> *Binding the work*
> *Binding the sport*
> *Binding the north, center, and south*
> *To triumph Peruvians…*

I'm here to tell you it sounds all kinds of splendid played on a phone, backed by the shorebreak at Casa Tudela.

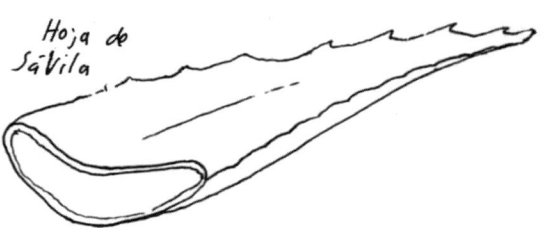

En Baja

A recent John Comer show in San Jose del Cabo, Baja Sur, Mexico.

From *The Surfer's Journal*, Volume 24, Number 6, 2015

"Back home," John Comer says, "I'd never paint at noon. But here the vocabulary changes."

For plein air master Comer, "back home" summons the suede-napped Mediterranean light of Alta California. The sandstone bluffs, the coastal ranchlands, the offshore islands. Contrasted with his current billet in Baja Sur, the northern territory is abundant with wind-brushed grasses, the coastal live oaks providing green relief. Golden hour illuminates the region with a viscous, honeyed density. The nearshore Pacific works as nature's ultimate complement, amplifying the values of the foliage in these *vaquero* pastorals. Alta California is where Comer made his bones.

As an outstanding member of the Oak Group, a Santa Barbara-based clutch of painting preservationists, it has been Comer's privilege to channel pure visions of the landscape to those who might benefit from well-crafted reminders. The Group has charged themselves with recording the baseline visuals of that region: the headlands, the uplifted coastal ranges, the chaparral hills.

The desired result can't be affected by mincing, merely decorative examples of living-room expressionism. What is needed are works eliciting a response, a call to action. What is needed, if we might dip into the vulgar Latin, are works with *cojones*.

In Comer's experience, painting isn't an occupation, let alone a dalliance. Indeed, even naming it as a calling falls short.

"Read Pablo Neruda's 'The Poet's Obligation,'" Comer says. It's a trick of fortune to have Neruda speak for you. Viewing

Comer's collected works, you find that the reference does not overreach. The poem by the canonic Chilean speaks to providing a service, offering visions of the sea to those far from its influence, both literally and metaphorically.

Now living in the Cape region of Southern Baja, Comer takes the obligation as seriously as ever. Here, along with the other desert creatures, Comer is active in *la madrugada*, the gray light before the dawn. A time to slow-troll up the dirt road to a dependable reef. The morning's prospects resolve as his truck settles on the beach berm, a 200-degree view of the cobbled almost-point commanding his attention. A handful of others pull up at various favored parking spots, eyes trained as the rays finally pour over the mountains behind, front lighting the ocean and snapping it to attention. Looking south, you can follow the windswell's passage down the coast, folding raggedly past sandbars, stacking up against rocky points, and rushing up into channeled guzzles, some sort of sense memory aiming the racing water toward estuarine *huertas*.

It's springtime, and the reef is off its feed. This time of year, it's more expected than deflating. The ritual surf check complete, he is freed to loose himself on the studio. Returning up the dirt road to his handmade, humbly artisanal *casita*, Comer leaves his sandals at the door and walks into the cool, plastered interior.

In the studio, easels hold works in progress. The space begs study, overfilled with elements of the working artist's kit. A stack of sketched renderings cover a surface, minimal marks capturing the skeletal structure of the land. Remarking on their starkness, Comer notes that simplicity is crucial and, perhaps referencing some old blues homily, sometimes one note is all you need.

"Drawing," says Comer, "is the key. Without that key, you don't get to come in."

Moving on to a stack of completed recent works, the paintings show that drafting skills are just the beginning. The finished works are layered with interest and information far, far beyond the simple blocking of the drawn composition. They show nothing less than the land come alive, the ocean throbbing then laying back.

As they have in California, Comer's desert works have found a serious following in Baja. He's represented by two Mexican galleries: the long-established, artist-owned Galería Logan, and the site of his recent powerhouse show *En Baja*, Galería de Ida Victoria.

The collected works seen in the *En Baja* show are, in the literal sense of the word, essential. As a visual textbook regarding the truths of the country, they speak for the non-human fabric of the land. The overall impact hits with the weight of a deer slug, but isn't always pretty in the traditional sense. The work documents a hard place seen in hard light but with priceless, timeless rewards hidden in the decomposed granite.

Comer has pointed views on it all.

"The light here is different. We're on the Tropic of Cancer. At midday, there is nowhere I've seen that is more shadowless. But there is illumination. I'm exercising new ways, for me, of conveying information. There's a desert brilliance. That's what I embrace, because it's something that is representative of the place. One thing I've always adhered to: Painting *must* be regional. It *must* be specific. That's what makes it universal."

If you have spent time at the Cape poking around the backcountry at different times of days and in different seasons, surfing the feathering point waves of the Mar, feeling the more direct, unrefracted energy of the Pacific side, you'll relate to Comer's work. If you've walked the arroyos—boots crunching over the alluvia, smelling the herbal gobernadora and jojoba—the work might awaken in you a sort of homing instinct. The vultures in the dawn light, warming their joints on the arm of a cardon. The laced interplay of sizzling foam and clear water in the wake of a wave, conjuring Spanish master Sorolla. The poignancy of a trio of palms scratching out an existence in salted soil. Comer gets beyond aesthetics and into the soul of the Cape.

It's an obligational burden he's happy to take up. Spend any time with him and you find that he has no choice in the matter.

Riding Cowgirl

Off the East Cape on *Vaquera*.

From *The Bight*, Volume 3, Number 1, 2019

•

This piece is for fishermen with basic East Cape literacy. For those who have had the pleasure of staying at one of the old Baja Sur lodges like Punta Colorado (RIP), Rancho Buena Vista, Rancho Leonero (RIP), Punta Pescadero, or the handful of other storied destinations spread like Steinbeck pearls up the eastern lobe of the Cape.

It's for those with a working knowledge of the region's history as related by salt writers like the foundational Ray Cannon, the comprehensive Tom Miller, and the ubiquitous Gary Graham.

It's for those who have camped in the lee of Frailes and Pulmo or down at La Fortuna, throwing plugs or double-hauling for toro and roosters, living rough but happily under tarps with dry ice for the beer and leaps into the sea for heat relief.

It's for those who have made the zone an annual rite, the highlight of their year, something that inspires wistful mind-drifts throughout the sclerotic periods back in the crowds and unabated noise of the north.

If the reader is not a member of the tribes categorized above, they are perhaps better served by jumping to the end of this piece.

But for the rest of us, read on.

And while you read, be honest and nod if you've ever run the diagnostics:

When you're on the Cape, you imagine yourself living there seasonally or even full-time. You'd buy or build a simple place. Beachfront would be deluxe (but, then again, so would a Gulfstream G4 and a harem of Tapatías). You'd want your own skiff or small cruiser. Maybe a local-knowledge-rich deckhand on call so you don't have to fish alone. A bodega with plenty of secure storage for tackle. A small pool for cooling off post-fishing and pre-siesta. A nearby pueblo with a handful of markets, restaurants, and cantinas. A dependable truck *con doble traccion*.

So you tally it all up and realize you must have made some kind of mistake. You'd be looking at no less than a million dollars—about 80 million pesos today at the exchange in San Ysidro. And that's not even factoring in the myriad hassles of expat life. In the words of lyrical poet Kahlil Gibran, "Love me gently—with a hay hook."

"If only," you ask the gods, "there was a way to spoon the cream from the East Cape fishing experience. To occupy, on demand, one of the finest private-angler haciendas in the heart of Buena Vista. To access not just a boat and local knowledge, but a late-model Cabo 35 Flybridge with tournament-winning captains fluent in our guttural, business-based native tongue. To return with the kill-boxes swollen with tuna and wahoo and *pez fuerte*, the macerators quietly chewing up the fishes' dreams of freedom. To retreat to a quick plunge in a shaded freshwater oasis, and then to a stunningly sited, handsomely outfitted oceanfront house with a Mount Olympus view of the fleet and the fishing grounds."

This is where we introduce you to Mark and Jennifer Rayor, their fleet of war wagons, and their fishing retreat, Casa Front Row. Together, they run Jen Wren Sportfishing, and there's nothing quite like it. And we've been looking.

They came down in the '90s, completing their house in 2000 on a parcel he'd bought in 1997. Mark had retired early back in '91 and, using something like the thought progression sketched above, decided on the East Cape. (Before they built their house, they lived in another Buena Vista home, in which they had a shared interest.)

"Then the stock market crashed and cut me in half," he says. Yellow alert. Change of plans. The couple acquired PADI instructor certification and started a dive operation serving the local resorts, eventually working up to a four-panga fleet. On his one day off, Mark would pursue offshore fishing, his life's obsession. And the East Cape being what it is, offshore depths were less than a mile from his new front door. The purchase of *Jen Wren*, an Innovator 31, marked the establishment of a new level of quality on the East Cape.

Shortly thereafter, the Rayors broke ground on their beach parcel, building a custom home with an adjacent three-bedroom vacation dwelling and a gigantic barn of a bodega. Jennifer, a hair stylist, spec'd a small poolside *casita* for her new appointment-only salon. The general effect of the compound is understated but oversized, and independently self-sufficient. From the automatic ship-chain entry gate to the fuel truck to the Caterpillar loader to the fleet of Cabos bobbing on buoys just offshore, thoughtful solutions to challenging logistics are in evidence everywhere one looks.

Take Mark's refueling process. There are no fuel docks in Los Barriles. You're on your own. And with three flybridges running fully booked in-season, dieseling up is like staging an opera. First, Mark's mate (Diego, Polo, or both) backs one of the big girls stern-first against the beach, a sketchy scenario even under optimum conditions. Mark fires up the tanker truck and rumbles down the arroyo, steamrolling to the water's edge where the truck's momentum finally stops as it sinks into the sand. A hose is transferred to the waiting boat and the fill-up commences. Once topped off, Mark leaps on a quad and races up the arroyo to his giant Caterpillar tractor. This is the rescue vehicle for the tanker, which can't make it back to the ranch through the deep sand. Mark deftly chains the two together and drags the truck back to its home. They have it down to a science, and it's a *sano*, drip-free system. It's his front yard, after all.

We got an eyeful of what it really means to run a backcountry charter operation during a visit last May. Scenarios like the one just detailed make up the bulk of Mark's day. He never stops running. He is, as they say with affection in the region, *muy chingón*. One wonders if it's pride, old-school work ethic, or merely the demands of office, but the truth soon presents: Mark is totally obsessed. He blows the "living the dream" platitude to pieces and fishes like a madman. And like all the best operators, he loves nothing more than to share it.

We stay at Jen Wren's Casa Front Row, natch, up at dawn our first morning. Fifty-two steps across the sand to hop in the waiting dinghy. No waiting. No queuing up on a dock. We'll be riding on *Vaquera* (*Cowgirl*), Jen Wren's spit-shined pride. Where preparation is concerned, you'll never see its equal. The vessel bristles with every Accurate reel in the catalog, all matched with a phalanx of new rods. There isn't a dried blood spot on the boat, even under the gunnel caps. In the galley, the smell of Jen's chile verde lunch wafts. Within seconds, the big turbos fire up for the sprint to the bait boats, easily beating the fleet to the alpha spot.

Diego shouts up to the bridge, asking Mark how he'd like him to rig. "*Quieren divertido*," he answers. "They want to have fun." Diego grins, says "*Atun*," ties up the marlin lures, and sets up for yellowfin. In half an hour we're well offshore of Pescadero, and

Mark quickly glasses a pod of small dolphin on the run. Intercepting, it's one strike, then two, then we're stopped, then we're quadrupled. The grade is *divertido*-size, but they're wide open. If there's a better way to start the morning than plugging the boxes with sashimi in 40 minutes, have your people call my people.

Diego reminds Mark of some dope they'd heard about—a little rooster snap going on at El Cardonal—and Mark drops the hammers for the run back inshore. I go up the ladder to shoot the breeze, parking on the bench forward of the helm and, with some light prodding, Mark starts in.

"When I bought the Innovator, neighbors started chartering it," he said. "It wasn't full speed, but it was something. But as you get older you start liking a more comfortable boat. I heard about a Cabo for sale in La Paz and took Jen up to see it. She had been saying, 'No way you're buying another boat.' But when she walked into the salon, she said, 'I could really see us on this.' We bought it, and that's when the business *really* took off. That was around '09. I was pretty puckered up when I bought her, but she became the most in-demand boat on the East Cape. Jack Nilsen from Accurate Reels helped me a lot. He sort of mentored me and coached me to the point where we've become a brand."

The yuks from the tuna hit are just fading. We're soon slow-trolling 30 feet off the sand. Boom. Five small and one respectable *gallo* are quickly added to the tote board. We fish with micro Valiant 300s, perfect little tools for the task. The bite eventually slows, and thoughts turn to the recent wahoo that had been defying the spring season with their presence.

Up top again, Mark continues.

"I bought this boat, *Vaquera*, a couple of years ago. First year I had her, we ran over 100 days. All told, we now run 250- to

300-days a year. June and October are the toughest to book, the most popular. I can't control if the fish are going to bite or not. But I can control the service, the quality of the boat, and the environment that we fish in. We have the finest tackle money can buy, the finest electronics…"

I consider interrupting, fearing we're drifting into corporate portraiture—then I look around at the boat, the gear, Diego in constant motion changing out tackle on the deck. I realize that Mark's rap isn't PR. It's utterly true. He has spared no effort or expense to make this a pinnacle experience. He and his crew would be doing this if they had to pay *us* to fish. They're that hardcore.

The next day we race south to Colorado and pin on some barracuda for the fast troll. Polo, today's deckhand, chucks a mirrored piece of two-by-four over the side, and when it turns in the wake and catches the sun it strobes hard, sending flashes 50 yards underwater. The undeniable science of Polo is confirmed when, moments later, a wahoo bites and proceeds to go dipshit at about 80 mph. I manage to keep things tight and boat my first skin. It's a solid fish in the high 40s. I wouldn't care if it was in the high 40 ounces. I've wanted one forever, and they've always eluded me.

Mark knew I'd had 'hoo on the brain and slapped me five. "The Sea of Cortez makes my job too easy," he says. I know better. From the immaculate fleet, to the fueling exercises, to the training of his crack crew, to the houses on the bluff, the whole Jen Wren operation exemplifies what happens when hard work and a sharp plan merge.

"Look," Mark says. "The key to the whole thing is this: I built this out the way I'd want it if I came down. I didn't copy anything from the lodges or anyone else. I just know the kind of boats I like to fish. When we built Casa Front Row, we built it as a family home for people to enjoy, not as a rental. The finishes, the furniture—everything is top end and comfortable. I'm not especially money motivated, though we do fine. I'm motivated by the challenge of building the best quality and experience around."

I raise my bottle in a genuine toast as we plow north back to the barn, a variety pack of fish in the box. Then I ask him about what I'd been told was his personal obsession: fishing for broadbill.

"Well," he says, "it's the challenge thing. Most fishermen never see one in a lifetime. When I don't have clients, that's what we're doing. Making bait, then going long. We drive past everything. Dorado. Marlin. Porpoise. We just have swordfish in mind, and we have blinders on. And you have to pay your dues. The more miles we log, the more time we spend out there, the better the odds are that I'm going to find one. It's like a needle in a haystack, though. I've never had a client willing to try those odds. It's hard to tell someone we have a good shot."

Back at the Casa, I survey the view, recounting the past few days, and come to a bonehead-simple conclusion: If someone wanted to try on the East Cape life from the perspective of a thoroughly dialed fisherman, they could do no better than to package up with Jen Wren. It isn't free, but the value is inarguable. The combination of the Rayors' hospitality, the respectful privacy they offer their guests, the *afición* and accomplishment of Mark and crew on the water—a stay here could easily steel one's resolve to spend as many days a year in the zone as possible.

Punta Impresario

Israel Preciado is driven by his Punta Mita beginnings—and an improbably detailed account of a midnight border crossing.

From *The Surfer's Journal*, Volume 32, Number 2, 2023

•

"I won't tell you what we used to use this arroyo for," says Israel Preciado, visibly shuddering. "I haven't been exactly here since they built this place. They did a nice job."

We're at El Surf Club at Punta Mita in the Mexican state of Nayarit, reclining on pillowed davenports with a pair of Maestro Dobel rocks in hand, one of those excellent *cristalino* tequilas grown and distilled up the hill in, well, Tequila. The surf sounds softly. The DJ, seeing us conducting this interview, has thoughtfully toggled back that reggaeton paean to May-September romance, "Mayores."

I tell Preciado that I haven't been exactly here, as he calls it, since 1980, when he was a mere egg. I'd hitchhiked up the point in the bed of a coconut truck. There wasn't a single place to stay, so we slept on the wooden tables of a seaside ramada on the beak of the point. The fishermen took us in. They weren't used to interloping gringo "tourists" and extended all available witchery and grace to keep us there. This included extra portions at mealtime. There was soft conversation regarding the nearby coral point wave, which they told us that some Texans occasionally surfed. They showed us how to hang a pink murex from the back of a chair until the little muscle relaxed, dropping its shell to the ground, the meat pulsing as it dangled from a fishhook.

That same cove is now noted for its "Tail of the Whale" golf hole, where one lobs one's ball onto the only island green in the world. Things change in 42 years. I recently told this story to a millionaire Chilango who had tripled his fortune in the bottled-oxygen business thanks to the pandemic. "I hope you bought land," he said. I told him I was a writing major then, living off the long con of student loans and Pell grants. I couldn't have financed a Crockpot.

We had marched across the prickly savannah to El Faro back then. It was hip-high, hard offshore, breaking with a snap on coral cobble. Difficult sledding on a swap-meet 6'10" Brewer pin. I'd purchased that $10 unit as a rock board for high-tide PB Point, rightly figuring that it would be at home in the hold of some Tres Estrellas bus.

Preciado indulges my memory trip politely. He's relaxed now. I typically try to have "antianxiety meds" at hand for interview subjects: fine tequila, American Spirit blues, a recent issue of the magazine, or something rare from the warehouse. On this occasion, all four are appreciated.

Preciado—called "Krusty" by his buddies for his *Simpsons* clown smile—has a lot going on. He's a part-time pro longboarder, real estate salesman, restaurant owner, and founder of the Mexi Log Fest, a traditional longboarding—née logging—event hugely popular among the 9-foot-plus set for its lack of pro-surf corniness. The surfers come to Mexico for the freedom, the warmth, and the party. It's Preciado's mission to supply those benefits.

These affairs are a favored stop on what passes for a classic surfing circuit. The World Surf League has a longboard tour, though with only three contests last year it stretches anyone's definition. Joel Tudor's Vans Duct Tape Invitational is the coin of the realm, influence-wise. Tudor is a fan and supporter of Preciado's program, going so far as collaborating to make the Mexi Log Fest Duct Tape–approved. This has been huge for Preciado in terms of visibility. That said, his long-standing relationship with the Austin, Texas, garment firm Howler Brothers provides the event its primary sponsor. "We are family," he says. "And family never goes away."

I ask him if his ambition is common among his friends. He doesn't quite answer my question. "I have a girlfriend and daughter," he says. Then he asks me if I know what a Malinche is. I've skimmed Bancroft's *The Conquest of Mexico*, and I answer that she was the beautiful *amante* and *guía* of Hernán Cortés, considered a traitor by those who might have forgotten that Montezuma had enslaved her people. To this day, the name is shorthand for Mexicans who sell out to foreigners. He says that some people in town call him that epithet.

"But it's kind of crazy," he says. "Since the first event, the festival was made to show people the talent of [Latin American] surfers. Surfers from Michoacán and Guerrero. South and Central America. Guys and girls who don't normally get the exposure. I started surfing here with my buddy, a local legend, Josue Villegas Almazan. He is like my mentor, and I am thankful for him for all the guidance he gave me in the water and all the expertise. I'm 41 years old and I was born in Mexico City. My parents were already living here in the area, in Puerto Vallarta, Punta Mita, this area, and I basically grew up, like, right here. It is kind of funny: The guys from Sayulita say I'm from Punta Mita, and the Mita guys consider me a Sayulita dude. But, well, I first moved to Sayulita when I was 4 years old, so it is just kind of hard for me to answer. In the end, I don't really care where I'm from."

Our waiter arrives with a tray of reinforcements. The afternoon light plays across the Bay of Flags, and Preciado's attention is drawn to the south. He mentions some favored spots below

Puerto Vallarta. He studies our immediate surroundings and registers appreciation. "This is pretty cool, man. Because, I mean, honestly, I come here to surf here, but I don't really look around to the umbrella zone, you know? I used to go fishing and spearfishing here. It is pretty good to have, like, a sick spot like this, you know? Whether it is to chill and then you can walk over there and then you see the tourists, you catch a few waves, and, like, I mean, I never thought it was going to turn like that in this area."

I ask him about his obvious interest in organized surfing. He takes a big breath. He'll need it. He's told the tale before. Over the years, the oratorical POV has jumped around, but with a clearing of his throat he jumps in: "So the whole inspiration of [the Mexi Log Fest] was this kid, this skinny kid that wanted to become a professional longboarder, but he came from a really poor family—where it is hard to qualify to be accepted in the United States to get your visa. So this kid has just heard from other friends of his that there are other ways to go across the border and make your dream come true. And he'd met this shaper from California who wrote a letter for him that said he should come and do the competitions. So he manages his way up to the border.

"He tried to apply for his visa at the consulate in Tijuana, and they said, like, 'No, kid, you have to go back [to] wherever you are from. You have to apply for it and do the process.' And he was like, 'Well, I just want to go surf. I want to be a pro surfer. I don't want to go to work. I don't want to take anyone's job.'

"Somehow, he managed to get some money from friends, and then he just went and stayed the night in a pretty sketchy part of Playas de Tijuana. He told me he was trying to sleep, you know? Just trying to sleep, and his window looked over the beach and it was pitch black. And he would sneak out of the window and there [were] all these noises and all these silhouettes, you know, like moms saying goodbye to their kids because they were about to cross the border illegally.

"He could smell the burning of plastic when people were cooking food on the beach before they made the journey to the other side. So, he was scared as fuck. He told himself, 'If I don't give it a try, I'm going to live the rest of my life not knowing if I could make it or not.'

"So he stripped all his clothes, taped on $400 that his friends gave him, and put a few phone numbers *entre nalgas*. He put his green boardshorts on—like, so green you can see them for miles—and jumped into the ocean with his board. And it was cold as fuck, as cold as he ever felt water in his life.

"He was just going through whitewater, whitewater, whitewater. Finally, he makes it so far out that he can't even feel the waves. So off he goes—paddle, paddle. He was in really good shape back then. And he keeps on paddling and that's when he starts hearing the helicopters. Looking to the beach, he can see immigrants crossing and just, like, running, running, running, running, and he can see the border patrol guys there waiting for them, waiting for the prey, you know? It was just so bizarre, so weird for him to watch that—like the guys were just sort of video game hunting, just to see how many of them they could collect at once.

"He told me he was going to meet a friend on the Imperial Beach pier. He landed there and he made his way up to the beach. The next thing he heard was someone screaming, 'Get on your knees, get on your knees!' Nowhere for him to run.

"The border patrol guy looked at him with the flashlight and said, 'Kid, what are you doing here? Where are your parents?'

And he was like, 'Well, I'm by myself. I'm just trying to become a professional longboarder.'

"They arrested him and took him down for deportation. That's when he told me his new dream: to make the coolest longboard contest he could someday. I decided to help him."

With a half-dozen festivals under his belt in a few Mexican locations, Preciado is pleased at having locked things down in his hometown. Mostly, he says he loves surfing here. He's been lucky to have traveled broadly and compares notes with ripping colleagues from Portugal, Spain, Uruguay, and a dozen other compass points. But his home base in Sayulita offers not only access to Mita's 270 degrees of swell and wind angle, but also the town-and-country vibe of the point at large.

A social animal, Preciado says he thrives in the mayhem of his environment—the chaos of surf schools, yoga and acai-bowl slingers, and that heady, mostly lampoonable space where New Age and Instagram converge. With the right wind, it has to smell like opportunity. As needed, he ejects to the wilds of a handful of as-yet-undeveloped honey holes where actual tubes offer themselves up. Minutes away, he and his gal can hose off and hit the *muy fresón* high-end eateries of Greater Punta Mita for a splurge.

As far as Vallarta proper goes, Preciado mostly gives it a miss. Too much traffic these days, though the cobbled streets and the charm of the old town still offer him a touch of Mexico Lindo. Most often, he sneaks into the bustling heart of the *turismo* during hurricane season, when neck-cracking pits present at the downtown beaches.

"So yes, I'm grateful to be here at home," he says. "The festival is growing, and I have a solid plan. The 'A' group of surfers will keep coming. They inspire the locals and international surfers who see them on TikTok and IG or whatever. Alex Knost, Jared Mell. The solid guys from Europe and Australia. The Mexican and [Latin American] surfers."

Preciado says that's where the surprise is. The known players get their first look at the crop of local style lords. The interplay—in the water, on the beach, and at night—is the secret to the whole thing. And then he breaks it all down and goes back to his hustles and his private surf life. And given the greater Mita resource—the variety of surf, the jungle, the nature, the commerce and opportunity—it's a life that suits him and his family well.

As we fold our tent for the afternoon, I ask him about the border-hopping kid. "Oh, him?" he says. "He finally did it all properly. He applied and got a US visa. Now he can go north and visit his girlfriend's family in Santa Cruz."

The Mangroves of Topolobampo

Fishing the estuaries of Sinaloa with Lupe López.

From *The Bight*, Volume 4, Number 1, 2024

•

August, Friday night, 2050 hours. The streets of Los Mochis, Sinaloa, are quiet. Even in the downtown business district, only the occasional car passes. I walk east in the direction of the Sierra Madre, somewhere out there in the dark. I'm used to SoCal, so I'm braced for all manner of night crawlers: whacked-out homeless, aggro partiers, miles of gridlocked traffic. But this is an agricultural city of the plain, and it rolls up the sidewalks after nine. It's also a fisherman's town, as Topolobampo on the eastern shore of the Mar de Cortés sits right down the road. Whatever you conjure when you think Sinaloa, this ain't it.

Up ahead a brightly lit, yellow-and-red food stand burns a hole in the night. Approaching, I see it's a bustling hive of activity. Cops, taxi drivers, families with children enjoying the cool of the late night. This is Hot Dogs Fatima, the unlikely headquarters of Lupe López, maybe the most recognizable mangrove fisherman in the state. As he has for decades, he's serving up Sinaloa-style hot dogs to a devoted crowd. The stand's success has led him to provide his family with a comfortable middle-class life. A house with a fine kitchen for his wife, a skilled regional cook. A university education for his children. And, more important for our story, the freedom to drag his boat down to the launch area a few days a week.

This is an auspicious sausage fest. I discovered Lupe via his YouTube channel. I'd been scouting likely estuaries along the coast of Sinaloa, and Bahía Santa María looked especially attractive. Delving deeper, I liked what I saw, with no shortage of pargo and snook on offer. Doing some online mapping from home, the estuaries looked huge, the mangroves constantly washed by ripping tides. It appeared healthy, dynamic. But you know how that goes. What I'd find would only reveal itself with boots on the ground. Would it be hopelessly fished out? Overwhelmed by desperate gillnetters? Polluted by infrastructure boondoggles?

Running comms with Lupe before the trip, I learned what I could about angling in the bays. It's mostly a bass-tackle fishery using 100- to 300-size low-profile baitcasters for pinpoint accuracy. Think skipping and splash casting. Hard baits mostly, but for the dawn topwater bite, poppers are the go. It's a boutique approach. Specialized. If you're into spotted bay bass and calico back home, this is your happy place. But while one might not choose to travel for spotties, light-tackle cuberas are another story. A five-pound Pacific doggie on a micro bass rod is all kinds of fun—like a largemouth that wants to clear the water and eat your throat.

The flight from Tijuana is about 90 minutes, and as you arc over Topolobampo on approach, the sheer range of the resource presents itself. The town looks like a scruffy Sausalito, bayfront and clinging to a hill. Endless cuts and channels disappear to the north and the giant Bahía Santa María. In the thousands of acres below, only a couple of boats could be seen. One of them might well be Lupe's.

The famous hot dog vendor is as rabid a fisherman as you'll find. As a teen, he pedaled his bike over an hour each way from Los Mochis to shore-pound the bay. These days, he lays up his own boats from homemade mother molds, makes all of his own baits, and knows every tidal creek on the coast. To fish with him is to gain entry to an entire fishing system. Technique, tackle, currents, and hidden holes are all in his purview. Twenty years in the esteros pays off.

"When I discovered the estuaries, it was all over. I committed totally," Lupe says. "I fell in love with the mangroves, starting with handlining. Little by little, I assembled some rod-and-reel tackle and experienced the thrill of tricking big fish with lures. It's my favorite way to fish the mangroves now. It can be difficult, but simply visiting *los mangles* is a relaxing and therapeutic experience for me."

Stands to reason. Mangroves work as the lungs of the coastal ecosystem, taking in nutrients from the sea and expelling carbon dioxide. Mangroves are also the pregnant belly of the organism, harboring its young until they're ready for the tooth-and-claw world beyond the bars. Beyond that, they are tranquil and quiet places. It's a calm fishing experience, akin to gliding down a lazy river. Shirt-off, barefoot, cold-Modelo-at-hand fishing. If you go for that.

Finishing the absurdly rich Fatima Dog (local beef, custom-baked roll, a pound of regional fixings), Lupe confirms our departure time. I walk the dark Sinaloa streets back for a nightcap at the hotel steakhouse.

Driving to Topolobampo at dawn, I have a chance to check out Lupe's rig. Corroded mini truck, 10-foot skiff nested in the bed, custom rod holder. A dialed, self-outfitted package of the kind you're more apt to see at the commercial basin back home. Banging our way to the beach launch, Lupe points out roadside mangrove cuts where he says you can grease a few quick pargo for lunch right out of your truck.

We pull up to the launch, where about a dozen trucks and trailers are staging. Coffee swilling and old two-strokes being goaded to life. Lupe has us splashed in mere seconds, and we're soon on plane toward a hidden entrance to a mangrove tunnel.

"The eastern Sea of Cortez starts with rivers," Lupe orates as he backs off of the tiller throttle. "Sinaloa is blessed by several rivers flowing from the Sierra to the Sea. That makes this Sonora/Sinaloa/Nayarit area unique. The river nutrients blend with the Sea and make the perfect place for mangroves. These are, in turn, home to thousands of species of marine animals. The mangroves provide life, that life provides us with food, and the whole system provides me with adventures."

That's a man who has boated about a million pargo and snook talking. I'm a little more crimped up. I need to get bit. On Lupe's suggestion, I'd flown down dry. He said he had the tackle so dialed I could only shortchange myself by bringing my gear. He'd packed a Plano box for me with a selection of his handmade lures, mostly little Rapala-style hard baits but also a handful of his poppers. He told me rods and reels weren't as important to him—whatever low-profile baitcasters and short, fast-action rods were available suited him fine.

The lures themself don't strike one as breakthroughs. They're mostly imitations of tried-and-true bass and inshore baits: X-Raps, Lucky Crafts, and jerkbaits, albeit with utterly photorealistic, hand-airbrushed finishes. These are precisely edited and sized, totally custom iterations designed for the mangrove waters from, say, Puerto Peñasco, Sonora, down toward Chacala, Nayarit, a zone comprising millions of acres of estero water. Surveying Lupe's tackle box, my Baja mind instantly had me craving a full set. There's no reason to believe his hyper-tuned lures wouldn't be lights-out from Morro Santo Domingo to Mag Bay.

"It all began when I stole a lure from my father and lost it," says Lupe. "I had some early success making metal jigs and soon enough I tried wood. The fact that I could fool fish with something I made by hand led me to my obsession. I began trying to make them more and more lifelike."

Lupe sells these "LoFish" lures in a few Sinaloan tackle shops. Predictably, area demand absorbs most of his output. I ask him how much stock he places on color.

"When the fish are active, it's irrelevant," he says. "When things get slow, though, I've found that matching the bait and responding to the water clarity is key. When I see a mullet or a shrimp jump, I try to imitate what the fish are eating. Also, when the water's clear, sardines and metallics work. When the water's clouded, I go bright. Fluorescent yellow, orange…"

Lupe coasts toward a memorized mark and starts casting. It's *media agua*, or mid-tide. The current is rushing in, pushing us quickly up the narrow channel. Casts are short, a hallmark of estero fishing. It's classic target shooting. You hear individual pargo hitting baitfish in the shade of the mangrove roots and throw to the boil. The trolling motor is used only for slight course corrections. The current provides a magic carpet ride as we ghost along at a couple of knots. You can cover a lot of water very quickly. Imitating Lupe's splash casting proves effective, and we're both on the board on the first drift. Casting into the tangled roots takes a toll, and getting hung up is part of the program.

The mangroves are indeed beautiful. The green walls absorb sound, with only a cicada hum and the line peeling off the reels making any noise at all. The mangroves are a healthy looking, saturated olive green. Every 200-or-so leaves is dead, giving the entire "forest" an uncanny, uniform appeal. By nine o'clock in the morning, the summer sun is reaching into the low 90s. There's no shade, and it's good to be inches above the water.

This is three-casts-a-minute territory, and the tiny reels and short rods—6'6" or so—suddenly make sense. We find ourselves in the slow season, coughing up a single pargo—gray, colorado, and cubera—on every third drift or so. It's also early for snook, though we turned up a couple. It's classic table fishing, and the fact that we're in a world heritage site of gastronomy—Sinaloa seafood and *mariscos*—has me double enthused on what will come: *aguachile* of shrimp, snapper, and robalo.

Deeper and deeper we push as we ride the tide. We pass the occasional beach clearing, the dry land carpeted with zacate grass. The odd small mountain drops down to the water's edge, looking like something from a John Ford western. Still we cast. Lupe sees something that has him grabbing his popping outfit. He casts 30 yards into the center of the channel, lets it rest, then gives it a rip. Another pause. *Whoomph*. A pargo destroys the thing, going on a short, intense run. The bite lasts for five minutes, and I'm stoked to manage a cubera on one of Lupe's handmade poppers.

We've worked our way from an area called Maviri into Bahía Santa María, a huge complex of canals and oxbows. There are dolphin hammering bait here, and with the breeze shifts you can hear the wind wave of the Cortés breaking beyond the bar. Late summer requires that one push deeper to find any numbers. Sinaloa fishing, Lupe says, is best from September to January, coming totally uncorked during shrimp season. The world's number-one producer of wild shrimp, the state bird might as well be the famously rusted trawlers of Mazatlán.

Back in Los Mochis by three o'clock in the afternoon, I hose off with a plunge in the hotel pool while Lupe heads home to butcher pargo. I've been invited to his house for dinner with his family. This turns out to be a highlight of the stay, not just for the cold "casserole" of snapper and shrimp, but for the window into Sinaloa middle-class life. Already known for their graciousness and hospitality, Sinaloans raise the bar on Mexican warmth. A solo traveler is embraced without reservation, invited into the family to embarrass himself with his "Me Tarzan" Spanish. As usual, street-level insertion into a misunderstood location proved deadly to prejudice. And even in this overpopulated, blown-out world, Southern California's relative adjacency to the Mexican coast and its diverse fisheries proves a surprise for those willing to dig a little.

Mr. Mayor, the Floor is Yours

Interview: Serge Dedina

•

I met the current mayor of Imperial Beach—the southwestern-most city in the US—back in 1994. He had just completed a doctoral thesis resulting in the inclusion of a remote gray whale nursery in the El Vizcaíno Biosphere Reserve in Baja. This meeting led to the publication of one of Dedina's first non-academic works, a feature on the big-wave spot called the Tijuana Sloughs. We maintained casual correspondence over the decades. Mostly, though, we kept to our hustles: Dedina at the cross-border conservation group WILDCOAST, and me at the inkpot.

In 2007, we became reacquainted in earnest. A handful of friends had formed a loose-knit group based on a shared, lifelong *afición* for a particular stretch of Lower California coastline. One of us was among the first to ever ride a wave there in the mid-1960s. Another had once hand built a stone cabin on one of the beaches, living by his lonesome through all seasons, learning the region down to the atomic level. Yet another, a pilot, had worked with the Flying Samaritans, bringing health services to remote ranchos. All had spent hundreds upon hundreds of days there, even in the surf-free months.

In the late '80s, a road was graded along that coast. Grueling two-track gave way to comparatively high-speed travel. The rush was on. The new roadbed offered vistas of heretofore-unseen coves. By 1995, a solid holiday swell at a mainframe point might see 30 campsites.

Those with history in Baja could read the tea leaves. Six hundred miles south, grading of the East Cape's Camino Costero Rural had led to real estate speculation, commerce, fenced-off beaches, and a profound insult to classical rural Baja life—and the environment on which it depended.

With only a scant handful of fisherman-ranchers living full-time on *this* 80-mile stretch of coastline, getting ahead of the onslaught felt plausible. The group charged me with reaching out to Dedina. While he had a long and successful conservation record on the peninsula, he was mostly unfamiliar with the north-central region. That did little to dissuade him. He met us in a humble backyard in Leucadia's Tortilla Flats barrio, where he presented a plan to lock down the entire coastline, soup to nuts, against future development. Surveys, title discovery, negotiations, outreach and education, management, and, of course, funding—all were accounted for. The presentation was streamlined and clear, speaking to Dedina's frictionless, high-velocity approach. A handful of the crew started the ball rolling by converting the titles to their privately held land into a conservation easement—a selfless show of faith. This game was afoot.

I accepted an unpaid position as *Asesor del Proyecto*—or project advisor—prioritizing headlands based on geographical charisma, objective beauty, and surf appeal. Basically, IDing the spots people might first try to purchase. WILDCOAST quickly bolstered these calls with actual science, shading in those parcels with anything resembling a wetland or attractive natural resources. A friend and I guided Dedina for his first real look at what came to be called the Lost Coast Project. Our original crew winced a little at the idea of a naming convention. We hoped for a "first do no harm" scenario operating on the down-low. It was, after all, fellow surfers who invariably privatized and overcrowded every honey hole from K-38 to Punta Pequeña. *No entran moscas*, the old *dicho* says, *en boca cerrado*. Flies don't enter a closed mouth. Dedina, rightfully, wasn't thinking that way. He was shopping for checks with no less than six zeros on them. And he got them. Quickly. But he also quietly intuited the dangers of putting anything on blast.

To date, the project has protected, for as close as anyone can come to perpetuity, 36.5 miles and 51,795 acres of central Baja coastline. Yes, carpetbaggers from *el otro lado* mine tonnage of beach cobble for the US landscape market. Some try to run for-profit 4x4 surf tours. Others stage banal, permit-free commercial photo shoots in the region. Social media posts bust the zone in ways that make old-time surf media appear almost saintly. But for the most part, experiencing the vibrational sanctity of a true coastal wilderness finds most folks checking their base instincts. And, thanks in large part to our mayoral subject, truly rapacious development will be legally held at bay for many lifetimes.

Dedina has, to my eye, changed little in these 25 years. He still speaks at volume with a rapid-fire command of both city-council English and *junta-ejidatario* Spanish. Tall and telegenic, he usually sports some variant of a Prince Valiant haircut. If he comes on a little strong—a trifle messianic—it can be attributed to his principle-fueled agendas. Especially, one will find, in defending his hometown against all manner of vile assaults. One wonders how he might scale this recently discovered gift for politics. For now, though, we'll keep it local.

SH: What makes Imperial Beach a unique surf town, from a national perspective?

SD: We're one of the last working-class beach towns left in Southern California. It's what many of our classic surf cities used to be like, after World War II through the '60s, until the coastal zone became too expensive for the average surfer. Our cultural diversity and location on the border give IB a different feel. We have a binational crew surfing on both sides of the border who are locals in IB and Baja. That can have its advantages when you're paddling out in Rosarito Beach or San Miguel and you see friendly faces in the lineup.

SH: Are the Tijuana Sloughs still a "thing," with guys hitting it up on bomber days?

SD: It's always been an underground spot, but it reached a zenith in the 1940s and '50s with IB legend and lifeguard Dempsey Holder. He surfed there with [Bob] Simmons, Pat Curren, and many more [legends]. It's notoriously fickle and rarely breaks way outside anymore. Combine that with horrendous pollution, and we're lucky to surf there a few times a year. That's a bummer, as there is nowhere I'd rather surf with lifelong friends and especially my sons, who grew up surfing there.

SH: How has the IB surf scene changed since your youth?

SD: I started surfing in 1977, when I was 13, and IB was full-on 1970s SoCal gritty surf culture—not unlike the HB from Kem Nunn's *Tapping the Source* and Venice/Santa Monica as depicted in *Dogtown and Z-Boys*. That changed at the very end of the '70s and into the '80s with a more dynamic and progressive surf scene and the surfing dominance of Glen and Mark Gould, Kelly Kraus, Dave and Jim Montalbano, Mike and Terry Gillard, Ricky Coronado, Dave Parra, Jim Sullivan, Aaron Chase, Alan

Cleland—made famous being featured on a *Surfer* two-page spread of an epic IB barrel—and many others. The IB scene was well documented by Aaron Chang, who grew up here. However, today the ocean pollution crisis has taken a huge toll.

SH: For those who don't know the situation, describe the Rio Tijuana sewage issue.

SD: Unfortunately, the significant growth of Tijuana combined with its dilapidated and failing sewage-treatment system has resulted in an ocean pollution crisis that regularly closes beaches from Rosarito northward to Coronado [in the US]. Whether it's non-stop sewage pump-station breakdowns, rain-caused collector pipe collapses, or the more than 130 points where toxic waste and sewage are being dumped into the Tijuana River, it can kill water quality for up to 20 miles or more on both sides of the border. The City of Imperial Beach, along with the state of California, Port of San Diego, and the cities of Chula Vista and San Diego, as well as the Surfrider Foundation, all sued the US federal government for violations of the Clean Water Act in the Tijuana River Valley. We just want the feds to build infrastructure to divert cross-border sewage flows back into the sewer system. We're also constantly working on both sides of the border to aggressively push officials at every level of government to fix this very fixable mess.

SH: How has the transition to city government gone? Has anything taken you by surprise about the process?

SD: Being the mayor of IB has been an incredibly rewarding experience. I'm grateful to have the support of a fantastic city council, which also includes three surfers—Paloma Aguirre, Mark

West, and Bobby Patton, who was an IB ripper in the '80s—as well as city staff and residents who have supported our efforts to improve every corner of the city. Sometimes I'm amazed about how fast we can get things done, and then other times, as in the case of the border pollution crisis, you see how problems are magnified by a "can't do" philosophy at every level of government. It would be the equivalent of having a bunch of people on the beach telling you constantly that padding out is impossible. You just have to ignore them, paddle out, and catch waves.

SH: Is local government as divisive as what we see in the national landscape?

SD: It can be, but we've focused on projects that bring people together.

SH: What are the biggest issues facing US coastal towns today?

SD: Climate change/sea level rise, affordable housing, and coastal pollution/development.

SH: How do you propose we address those?

SD: For climate change and sea level rise, we have to commit to addressing coastal erosion using natural climate solutions, protecting and restoring all of our natural ecosystems to make them more resilient, and continue to permit unfettered coastal access for all. So the more we can restore our wetlands and watersheds and protect our reefs and kelp forests—the more we can avoid things like breakwaters and seawalls, and work with nature instead of against it—the better. Rising seas and erosion are a huge threat to surf spots globally. I was amazed when I surfed in Chile, Nicaragua, and Oaxaca to see the major damage that increasingly stronger Southern Hemisphere storms are having on beaches in regions that are pretty undeveloped. Throw in badly planned coastal development as well as increasing pollution, especially in the developing world, and we're seeing some significant damage to coastlines. So we can develop and grow economically, we just have to respect and restore all of our natural areas on the planet and focus on sustainable development in a way that minimizes our impact to the environment—which is totally doable. In terms of affordable housing, California beach cities—and cities like Sydney are similar—have become unaffordable for 99.9 percent of the population. We've created a de facto apartheid system of housing, where only the wealthy can afford to live near the coast. That has to change, and we're all going to have to build more affordable housing or the state of California is going to force cities to do it.

SH: What does a typical Tuesday look like for you?

SD: For my work at WILDCOAST, a typical day may involve visiting our Ensenada office. That entails a dawn-patrol run to San Miguel, paddling out in the dark for what can generally be a pretty fun session. I'll be joined by Zach Plopper from our San Diego office, as well as Eduardo Najera who runs our Mexico program and lives nearby. We'll eat breakfast at Café Toya in Sauzal, which is a full-on surfer hangout, or the newer Escama Gastro Café. We'll then meet with our staff and review our projects at our office. Then it's time for lunch. If we're in a hurry, we'll grab tacos at El Trailero or, if we have more time, we'll hit up Boules or Muelle 3—a must-stop after a day surfing Todos—for a meal with our WILDCOAST team.

SH: How's surfing doing from an ocean conservation POV? Do we seem to be more engaged these days or less, compared to, say, the 1980s...

SD: I'm really impressed with the growing Global Wave movement. That's the coalition of organizations from around the world committed to preserving waves and beaches. I'm really stoked that WILDCOAST works closely with the Surfrider Foundation and Save The Waves and all the other fantastic ocean conservation organizations, especially those from Peru, Chile, Mexico, Europe, Australia, and New Zealand. I'm also thankful to SIMA for its support of ocean conservation via the Waterman's Ball. I'm a big believer in the surfing-reserve movement. But we have more challenges than ever. It's critical that we have organized teams of surfers dedicated to preserving the natural integrity of our surf spots, which are also critical fish habitats, marine ecosystems, and can be economic drivers of local economies. We need to continue supporting an all-of-the-above conservation strategy and build the capacity of organizations around the world to preserve our shorelines—and make sure that we have access to them.

SH: San Diego at three million people, Tijuana at about two million. It's a region that surpassed, arguably, its carrying capacity half a century ago. What gives you hope as a surfer? As a mayor?

SD: We're learning how to be more sustainable and reduce our impacts to the environment. We have to continue pressing to increase green infrastructure to reduce stormwater pollution, conserve and restore our green and blue open spaces, and reduce emissions so that we have clean air and water. The sustainable-city movement is here in a big way. One of the things we need to continually address is whether we want people living in cities or building new suburban developments in the backcountry or in the coastal open space that is, for now, undeveloped. While I'm an optimist, we need strong leadership at every level in government and the private sector to push to be both economically and environmentally sustainable.

Tentative in Manabí

A flâneur's search for a lid—and sand-sucking drainers—in Ecuador.

From *The Surfer's Journal*, Volume 33, Number 4, 2024

•

I needed a hat. Let me explain: My working quiver doesn't travel well. Lifeguard atrocities. Park helmets (sisal piths favored by landscape workers). Sweat-stained Resistols.

All sensible choices for the desert and Med zones I tend to favor—Köppen climate zones B and C. Problem was, my 2023 docket was slammed with joints more Kipling than Ed Abbey. Monsoonal, *Aguirre, the Wrath of God* waypoints. Tampico. Holguín. Las Terrenas. The call was for something durable but not out of place in the *zócalo*. REI, avid-outdoorsman, recycled-synthetic lids? *Claro que no*. The obvious play was for something with a modest brim, yet wide enough for torrential night ops. Foldable and crushable. Something time-honored. Something Panama. Would I present as some Tony Montana manqué or, worse, a cruise-ship boomer? Fifteen years ago, I might have cared. Now, it's pure function lust.

A research tumble led me to Ecuador. "Panama hat" is a misnomer. The original, the finest, the *superfino*, all hail from a small town called Montecristi, where they are grown, woven, blocked, and shipped worldwide. Like everything exquisite and handmade, the pricing can be astronomical—thousands of dollars and up. Yet a perfectly fine roll-up in a small cedar tube—not much larger than a Toblerone chocolate bar—can be had for under $200 if you can teleport to Ecuador.

Toggling the map to Montecristi, near the central-coast tuna port of Manta, the scales fell from my eyes. I recalled the name. Manta used to be the home of a wave rivaling Chicama for length. Indeed, a friend once lived there as a fishing consultant in the '70s. He had surfed the screwfoot paradise at San Mateo before the harbor construction cut it in half.

Proceeding in the modern lazy manner, I had a look using the IG location feature. Clean blue waves fractalized on my phone screen. Tellingly, these were peaks I'd never seen or heard of before. The photos were all authored by a Francisco Herrera. I DMed him at once. Herrera said that no surf magazine had ever visited Manta. I booked a flight. I can't speak to how the big-cheese online dick swingers bird-dog travel stories, but weird curiosity with an overlay of horde avoidance has never done anyone dirty.

Señor Herrera was gracious and receptive. He invited me to Manta with no strings attached. He's a businessman in the bottled-water trade and a community pillar. His wife works in the mayor's office, and his brother is the national minister of transportation. He scheduled a hole so he could show me around. I knew the waves were there. I'd seen the shots. I was looking forward to boiling the bones of the Ecuadorian coast, swimming in the hazards and surprises and vegetable smells. That would not present any difficulty, said Herrera. Neither, from a look at his file, would an article. Hell, one could fill 20 pages with nary a word.

I started in Lima, Peru, my third visit there that year. That place has a hold on me. The two-hour flight to Guayaquil was routine, right down to the traditional Ring of Fire earthquake the city had experienced the day before. A fresh El Niño was also flooding the backfield with Old Testament downpours. Dropping out of the clouds, the reveal was shocking. The rancid-looking Rio Guayas was in flood, all manner of king-size flotsam—some of it recently deceased—threatening navigation. The city itself looked disassembled: an ad hoc, sopping warren of unplanned and ill-conceived structures tracking off to some drizzly vanishing point. Picture post-Katrina New Orleans. The runway lay under a scrim of standing water. The jet hydroplaned for a nauseating moment.

At the taxi stand, things failed to improve. Garbage piles. Gouts of sewage erupting from storm drains. Glued-out homeless patrolling just across the street. Guayaquil, to my none-too-delicate sensibilities, was a three-alarm hellhole.

I love such places. Presaging the social media rat-outs that had aided my research, a mentor of mine famously said, "In the future, the only adventure will be found in cities."

"Only" is a hell of a word, but he wasn't wrong. Freedom, anonymity, value, comfort (when you need it): All are on offer in most Latin American cities. US and Western European metros are hopelessly played, locked in a miasma of indefensible expense, news cycle me versus you, and the ennui borne by manufactured outrage. LatAm somehow defies such banal orthodoxy.

Whether posting up for three nights or three months, there's a recipe for success down south—a punch list. First, find the best old-school hotel bar in town. This will be your base of operations. Then, rout out a steakhouse/*parrilla*/*churrascaria*. Next, locate a barber, a driver, and a local fixer. This last can double as a bodyguard if you don't know how to take a knife away from someone. That's it. Grease all of these providers liberally. Assuming you have working Spanish and common sense (phone stashed unless within a business; hotel keycard, currency, and a single non-debit credit card in front pocket; a full Zippo), you're good.

Herrera arranged for my driver, who arrived from distant Manta. An underworld pal hipped me to my fixer, whom we can call

Remilio. Remy was from Guayaquil. He'd immigrated to Miami, enlisted, and done two tours with the Marines. Martial life had stuck. He rolled with a buzzcut, a mil-spec backpack, and a telescoping, whiplike baton. That horrible thing lived in his pocket, never leaving his grip. Guns are illegal in Ecuador. Predictably, only crims and cops have them. Knives, too, are outlawed, but far more common. Remy had security papers, but was authorized for only the whip. He brandished it no fewer than three times on our walks. A shark can smell blood from a quarter mile away. Remy could smell something looking to spill ours from double that. I'm low-key vigilant, but Remy looked through walls. He told me that the baton had taken many pelts. I assured him that, like Ovid, I sang only of love and would not invite confrontation. He rolled his eyes and made me walk in the street, thus avoiding the doorways.

Two days later, I dropped down to the street outside my hotel to WhatsApp my driver for the trip to Manta. I sat on my carry-on outside the foyer. A vendor was on the curb, selling sundries from a cart. A grinning skell pedaled past him, playfully tossing an empty plastic water bottle. It bounced lightly off the head of the vendor, who immediately called after him, urging him to come back—as if he wanted to catch up with this friend from the streets.

When the cyclist returned and rolled to a stop, the vendor reached into his cart, withdrew a sharpened piece of rebar, and stabbed him in the liver. Falling off the bike, the skell clawed at his stomach, a confused look on his face. The city street was busy with pedestrians. None stopped. The cyclist continued to bleed out on the asphalt as my driver pulled up.

The drive to Manabí, Manta, and Herrera, toward the procurement of my hat, was uneventful but educational. Over the course of several hours, the driver related the story behind each *poblado* we drove through: These are mango orchards. Here they sell cheese bread. Notice all of the Chinese motorcycles the farmers use instead of horses. These wooden bowls they are selling are from native trees. Here is where the truckers stop for girls. This is Montecristi, and here is your hat vendor. And, right at the three-hour mark, here is Manta.

You could actually smell the difference between this oceanside city and the delta of Guayaquil. Manta is clean, salt-cured. Tuna clippers and an organized shipping terminal. Faint notes of nearby agriculture, loamy and rich. Restaurants clad in the trendy horizontal lumber, " ____&____ " style that was popular in the US a few years ago. *Pádel* clubs, players enjoying a cocktail between sets or chukkers or whatever they call them. Once free of Guayaquil, Ecuador took on a hopeful, commerce-driven glow.

I joined Herrera the next day at his Puríssima bottling plant. His justly placed civic pride was in full cry. He had a youthful face, a trace of mustache, and the resigned air of a man used to solving South American logistical issues.

"My friend," he told me, "Manta is really on the verge of great things."

Taking me to his upstairs office, he directed me to look out the window.

"That's the airport right there," he said. "They just announced the first international flights from Panama City. For the first time, surfers can fly without having to stop in Guayaquil or Quito."

Those familiar with the country know that most surfers concentrate their efforts well south of the city, in the Salina-to-Montañita zone. Herrera hopes that surf travelers will find his hometown the sort of undercover treasure that he was raised on.

"I started surfing in the late '80s on big boards my brothers had," Herrera said. "But I really got into bodyboarding. The best wave in town is El Escondido at Playa Murciélago. It's a full tube. It's a north- and west-swell spot, like most of the waves around here."

It's also the main beach in town, marked by a promenade and beach services. Beginners and townsfolk at El Medio beach look right into the maw when the refractory hell-wave is on the chew. Rabid spongers lock down the top-loaded beast with little conflict. The sand slab defies all but pro-level stand-up cats, and those are in short supply here. Herrera said that the jewel of the area is found just out of town, near a stretch of beachside villages. We made plans for a survey.

Driving south the next morning, we stopped at the overlook for the famed left at San Mateo. Inside of the jetty, clean, knee-high lefts defined the bar. If you blurred your eyes, you could fill in the point-of-yore's entirety and grasp what once was. In season, it still offers a mirror-image, Santa Barbara sandbar deal: sucking, hollow-as, backless pits. Watching this heritage spot, Herrera spoke about his start behind the lens.

"I started practicing photography at the beginning of the 2000s, with analog cameras and camcorders. It always remained a secondary activity for me, since the main thing was surfing good waves," he said. "With the arrival of better equipment in the digital era, I started getting more active. Taking photos and surfing mentally gives me a different perspective of the spots—the nature, the people, and the entire environment. This is why I greatly prefer surf landscape photography. I also take action photos, but I think a perfect lineup or a solitary peak surrounded by nature and magical conditions fills the soul."

He went on to catalog how he loved to document the setups we'd soon see: the precise swell and wind demands, how unpeopled they were, the opportunities for investment and how that would benefit the local economy. He wanted to make the best-possible impression of his home, overlooked for so many decades.

While my translation does him no service, Herrera was just that earnest-sounding in person. Every conversation was marked by a kind of relaxed fervor. I wanted to ask him if he was at all concerned about opening the floodgates, looking to drop personal experience. I told him that it's our mode to tread lightly, favoring allusion over guidebooks. He looked at me as if he'd never heard anything so absurd. Stepping back, you can see how the country has more important fat in the fire. Life-and-death shit. It's beyond national pride. It's more a matter of survival.

What might feel like chamber-of-commerce boosterism hits different in Ecuador, a country that has its work cut out for it. Security remains the prime concern. A record glut of coca in neighboring Colombia and Peru has attracted transnational players from Mexico to the Balkans. Then there's the crushing Venezuelan diaspora and its Tren de Arugua gangsters. The three have all but overtaken the country, assassinating politicos, taking control of prisons, and firehosing millions in bribes and influence peddling. For Herrera and his family, it's a hairball proposition. Tourism, surf or otherwise, is a rare ray of hope.

Descending from a cloud jungle half an hour later, we arrived in the little fishing town of San Lorenzo. Moments later, we were buzzed through the gate of the Keith Keller compound. An East Coast surfer with a modeling/acting background, Keller met his Ecuadorian wife in NYC. The lifelong surfer moved with her to her home country, launching a surfboard company featuring his shapes, Mineral Surfboards.

Behind the gate, a handful of hardwood-accented, custom two-story houses surrounded a cabana and swimming pool. The backdrop was lush, with swarms of butterflies and exotic birds flitting. Waves as seen in these accompanying photos lay down a dirt path. If I got mercantile and vulgar, you would laugh at the amount such an airbrushed van mural of a situation goes for. I'll write the figure on a slip of paper and pass it under the table.

We relaxed in the shade of the cabana, where Keller and Herrera exchanged news of a fresh swell. Their lovely wives, legs tucked under them, exchanged child-rearing reports with glasses of juice in their hands. It could have been a scene from anywhere green and happily lassitudinous: *White Mischief*-era Nairobi, or Pavones in the '80s.

Making plans for the remainder of the week in hail-of-vowels Spanish, I noted their concern for my impressions. They needn't have worried. The photography, as ever, would do the grunt work. Hat in hand, I remained along for the ride.

El Molino Viejo

(The Old Mill)

San Quintín, BCN.

From *The Bight*, Volume 2, Number 2, 2018

El Molino Viejo (The Old Mill)

•

Let's spec out an ultimate fisherman's watering hole. Grab a pencil. This is serious.

Since we're starting from scratch, no request is too absurd. Building codes, ridiculous construction fees, grotesque real estate costs—out the window.

First, let's put it on an actual dock. Forty paces from the cleats to the bar rail. With a view of a bay. And no tourists, hustlers, or squares. Tucked away is what I'm saying. If you're there at all, you're there to bend, drink, sleep, and repeat.

And the interior: No fake maritime crap or Wyland prints, okay? If you're gonna hang the place with nautical junk, make it real. Like, "buy an old salvaged Coronado Island ferry" real. Truck that old tub down Mex 1, tear it apart, and mount chunks of it throughout the joint—a boiler here, some creosote-coated timbers there, maybe the original *North Island* nameplate on the wall. And didn't Hector drag a brokeback panga into his yard from down the beach? Skilsaw that heap in half and mount the whole damn thing over the backbar.

Let's talk stemware. I'm over those pint glasses, aren't you? In fact, I'm over "craft." At least today. I'm in the mood for straight swilling. Lip-smacking, belt-straining, Forest Service-tanker drops of fire-dousing Mexican pilsner. So let's have tap heads of Indio, Tecate, and Bohemia. And serve it in giant glass tankards that leave six-ounce rings on the bar top.

Beer not your hustle? Two choices, both of them epic:

First, rum. Not Bacardi, not Ron Rico, not Myers or Mt. Gay. Not even Flor de Caña. We're going Cuban, holmes. Havana Club (pronounce it "cloob"), either three or five years old. You can't get it in the States for the exact same reason you can't smoke a real Bolivar Robusto or practice horizontal Pilates with a tube-topped *doctora* from Cienfuegos—the government doesn't want you to know what good is.

Second, tequila. Call it, we'll have it. Even a house brand.

Let's talk 502s. Nonstarter. Drinking and driving is for kooks and mouth breathers. You wanna take out some family coming home from the ice cream shop? End up in the joint with Kimbo Slice admiring your marbling? *Claro que no.* So here's the genius part: Let's put a cheap hotel…next door. And by cheap, I mean "15 bucks a head" cheap. "Sheets about a week newer than the Shroud of Turin" cheap. "Four twin-beds in a room" cheap. But clean! And with safe parking for your truck. And, while we're at it, let's put an entire second bar in the hotel. And for good measure, let's put a third about 100 yards away. For triple-crown events.

And when gray light gets the threadbare curtains glowing, how about a stumble downstairs to the dock, where a pleasant local *matrón* has hot coffee and breakfast burritos ready to go as the skiffs idle in the eddy.

We can dream, right?

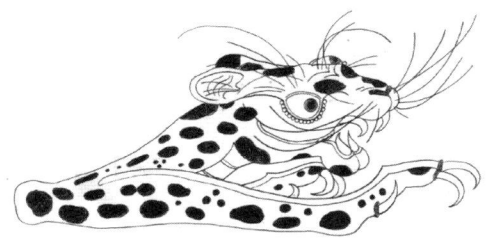

AKA Stoner's

How the original secret spot was overshadowed by time and inclination.

From *The Surfer's Journal*, Volume 28, Number 1, 2019

•

In the spring of 1964, Long Beach surfer and photographer Leo Hetzel scrambled up a rock balustrade in the state of Nayarit on the mainland of Mexico. Peering over the top, he copped the first surfer's view of a setup now known popularly as Stoner's. The lineup, as it is today, was a warm green cove infused with freshwater from the adjacent rivermouth just out of sight to the north. The atmosphere was silent, hot, and thick. Blinding-white thunderheads exploded over the inland sierra. A set of waves lurched upward like cereal boxes on a conveyor line and chased themselves toward a beach of yellow sand. Hetzel watched as the set traveled south around the next point toward Matanchén Bay.

Later that day, he told his pals what he'd found hidden around the corner from their annual holiday hangout. The following morning, the crew logged first tracks at what would be known for the next couple of years as "the secret spot." They didn't hide their discovery, but neither did they broadcast it. Back home, the various members of the crew did what surfers have done ever since, and their actions probably say as much about human nature as they do about our specific culture: Under direct questioning, some cast vague obfuscations, while inevitably others offered hard intel.

What happens to a dream realized? Once discovered, does one stop at perfection? Not if our past movements count for anything. Plotted on a graph, the life cycle of a surf spot usually describes a familiar "up and to the right" motif. The line spikes skyward, spurred by increased awareness and visitation, until carrying capacity is met, exceeded, and then merely endured. Many are wired to deal with it. Others complain bitterly. Some quietly move on, naively vowing that next time they'll hold their mud.

The prime example is, of course, Malibu. Postwar population dynamics transformed that cobbled heaven into a Malthusian dystopia by the 1950s. For the first time, surfers seeking even a hint of freedom had to look elsewhere. Malibu—indeed, Southern California—became not a destination but a place you left. Many of these refugees were seeking precisely what they'd lost: a wave like First Point.

And strangely, Stoner's—the spot that became a sort of avatar for tropical perfection in the '60s—now finds itself a forgotten backwater with relatively little surf visitation to speak of. Orphaned by a combination of new discoveries, a popular preference for hollow, performance-friendly waves, and a reputation for often unendurable living conditions, Hetzel's baby was effectively left on the hospital steps by 1970. The cycle of Mexican surf exploration invites study.

Los Angeles big-wave carnivore Greg Noll went wave hunting in Mexico expecting cold beer, cheap living, and some adventure. "In 1954 I was living and surfing in Mazatlán by myself," he says. "I stayed three months. It had everything I was looking for. I came in from surfing Lupe's [a left now referred to by local surfers as 'Camarones'] and an old guy came down to the shoreline to greet me. He was dressed like one of those Veracruz guys, you know, all in white, hat and all, like *The Treasure of the Sierra Madre*.

"He had a goddamned burro on a lead. A kid translated for him and told me the old man thought I was Jesus when he saw me standing on the water. He made the sign of the cross, and then very carefully he reached out with his goddamned hand shaking and he touched my board.

"That kid kept me company, 'cause he could speak English and Mexican [sic]. He told me if I left the beach with my shirt off the cops would haul me in. I stayed at the old Freeman Hotel at Olas Altas. I surfed out front and at that left point with the old Spanish fort. Bing Copeland named it 'Cannons' on his trip down there. I'd wrote to Bing and Yater and Rick Stoner, see, and they all came down the next year. Just exploring around the coast, I found San Blas. The wave at Matanchén Bay wasn't big, but it was perfect—long, crisp rides."

Like Malibu.

The following year, Noll returned to Mazatlán with a movie camera, documenting the Sinaloa shrimp port and its pleasant, if not world-class lefts. The resulting footage appeared in Noll's first *Search for Surf* film in 1957. Mexico, with all of its dark and colorful allure as portrayed in popular culture, found purchase in the minds of US coastal youth.

The 1,300-mile run from Southern California quickly became a rite of passage. Every swinging dick with decent wheels and a carny roll of pesos crossed the line, plunging south across the Sonoran Desert. But this was the early '60s, and that entire diaspora numbered in the dozens. In 1961, Leo Hetzel was one of them.

"Mazatlán was where we'd go for Christmas and spring break," says Hetzel. "Not the best time for waves, of course, but we got lucky once or twice and saw the potential. I liked Matanchén Bay enough to move there in 1965. I rented a dirt floor *palapa* on the point at Aticama and made friends in the town. They were lovely people. By that time there were a couple of surfers living around San Blas. Well, they were druggies more than surfers.

They'd be stoned in the morning, on speed in the afternoon, then on pills at night to go to sleep.

"We'd come down in VW buses, and the year I lived there John Fletcher—Herbie's brother—was with me. After I found the wave, we walked the animal trail through the jungle and surfed 'the secret spot' for the first time. It was head-high and good, but we were afraid of the rocks and rode conservatively. The waves were long and clean. The only people we saw were locals fishing from hollowed-out logs."

Hetzel couldn't have envisioned any sort of surf invasion taking place. The distance and expense, in time and treasure, were the first filters. The language barrier and parochialism were the others. And then there were the *jejenes*. And the mosquitoes. And the no-see-ums. Matanchén Bay is surrounded by an exquisite wetland, latticed with lagoons, creeks, and oxbows teeming with all manner of life. Indeed, the bulk of area tourism comprises bird fetishists and crocodile voyeurs. Insects are the state flower. Cumulus swarms descend at gray light, back off to tolerable in the midday heat, and then find their tallest gear in the evening. The place is defined by them.

As a surf resource, it's also defined by a narrow swell window. One could sit steaming and scratching for months on end waiting for something—anything—to wrap in. Which is just what a handful of early ferals did, especially during the draft years. For those lucky or stalwart enough to score swell, the main wave at Matanchén, Las Islitas, was the sort of experience one didn't soon forget. On a well-foiled period point-tanker, one could stall and dance around the pocket for upward of a mile, milking it until the perfect little crackler committed seppuku somewhere down near the Jalisco border.

Factor in a local per diem of five bucks a day, including all of the rotgut Orendain tequila and liberally seeded sierra sativa one could handle, and San Blas took on a certain "Graham Greene on food stamps" appeal.

The weed, in particular, became a raison d'etre for many early surf travelers. Grown in the mountains by Huichol farmers, it was cheap enough as to be nearly free. One hundred dollars worth would scarcely fit in the trunk of a '49 Plymouth. As such, early surf scammers beat their way north packed to the rocker panels with low-grade tonnage. At LA street prices for ounce lids, a successful run could net a surfer enough cash to float him for two years. A lot of bosses got fired, and a lot of surfers got to play all day.

By the middle to late '60s, San Blas found itself a waypoint on the hippie trail, discussed in the same ecstatic manner as Goa, Kandahar, and Cusco. In California, surfing was revved up, feeling its oats as a bona fide countercultural indicator. *Surfer* magazine, hungry to feed its audience's voracious appetite for new discoveries, dispatched ace photographer Ron Stoner to head south. While other surf travelers—Ron Pierrot, Peter Troy—had pushed away from the predictable California/Oz/Hawaii taxi ranks, Stoner's photos from Mazatlán and San Blas were lush and evocative enough to instantly become visual shorthand for surf exploration.

In a bullpen move that dollared out as a master stroke, *Surfer* editor Patrick McNulty paired the images with narrative illustrations from staff hippie/Rasputin, Rick Griffin. McNulty wrote the words himself. Despite Stoner and Griffin never having been to Mainland Mexico together—and the author never at all—the issue was a global hit. Stoner's '63 Mercury Comet wagon, stacked with signature models and a crew of attractive vagabonds, became an archetype for the wayfaring wave rider, and readers didn't have to squint to see Matanchén Bay as some sort of tropical First Point—an impossibly sexy and relatable proposition.

Interest piqued by the project, Griffin himself made a trip to San Blas a personal quest. That opportunity presented itself soon enough. "In 1966," says Griffin biographer Steve Barilotti, "Rick's wife, Ida, became pregnant. Rick fled fatherhood, sold his studio, and took off to Mexico. He went to Mazatlán first, ending up, of course, in San Blas. He sent postcards back with depictions of himself dodging crocodiles and bandidos. Ida reacted by giving birth, getting on a bus out of Tijuana, and presenting Rick with his daughter, Flavin, right there in his hammock."

Griffin, it seems, managed to pull it all off—with the intrepid assistance of Ida. He came home to California with sketchbooks brimming, fueling his future work with imagery redolent with Huichol shamans and stoic *campesinos*.

Interest in the region hit a boiling point with San Blas—and its nearby alternative Mexican Malibu, Faro de Mita—becoming number one on every Californian and Texan's hit parade.

For a brief moment, it almost got crowded. Almost.

Then, due mostly to the advent of the shortboard and partly to a natural urge to push south, seekers found themselves plunging deeper to hollower, more challenging waters. Almost instantly, sleepy Matanchén Bay found itself cuckolded by waves at La Ticla, Rio Nexpa, and Petacalco. San Blas pretty much went to sleep, and Hetzel's "secret spot" (presumptuously recast as "Stoner's" by the unwitting *Surfer* staff) retreated into the vines of memory.

Was there more to the story? There usually is. Surfing never really buries its legends—it keeps them in a cool room, hits them with some makeup, and stands them up for another generation to appreciate. And there was no way the current crop of longboard hustlers would overlook a mile-long point wave, was there?

I hadn't visited San Blas in over 30 years, and that trip had been a memory-lane rumble back when I was corrupting the girl who would become my wife. I used to spend time at Stoner's and had wanted to return. Somewhat sadistically, I saw it as a sort of pressure test. Could she hang? (And how, as it turned out.)

This past summer found me in need of some plasma-warm point crumblers. Being cognizant of reports that Stoner's was essentially a ghost wave only galvanized my interest. I'd put off this prodigal visit long enough. A Mexican national colleague, Mark Kronemeyer, picked me up in Mazatlán, and off we went. Driving south through miles of mango and blue agave fields, we crossed the river bridge into San Blas three hours later.

There were crocodiles in assorted sizes lolling in the mangrove breaks. The old town center had weathered well. The city fathers had passed some writ that had all the shopkeepers unifying their signage. It was vaguely quaint, lending a colonial charm to the pueblo I remembered as bedraggled. Then there was the Proustian scent of the place, the burning of damp coconut husks used to ward off the Transylvanian *jejenes*. Better than acceptable lodging was found in a restored hacienda.

The next morning we met a clutch of Kronemeyer's friends from Sayulita on the beach at the tip of Matanchén. Gathered there at dawn, swatting against the onslaught, I asked the crew what they expected to find out at the point. The waves where we had parked were utter dishwater and did nothing to instill confidence. Twenty-five-year-old Dylan Southworth, a fisherman's son raised in Nayarit, said they knew exactly what to expect up around the corner. Indeed, they make the trek regularly.

"We're looking for pretty specific conditions when we come up here," he explained. "The best deal is when a storm crosses the Mar de Cortés and aims some energy straight and hard into the bay."

We weren't quite so lucky, but came properly equipped. The previous day's surfing had shown that. The ad hoc group of surfers were well-versed in all conditions and were far from hidebound, board-wise. Southworth launched credible airs with little evident wave energy. Log-jammer Israel Preciado chose artful, section-connecting lines. Leila "Taquito" Takeda, Southworth's chica, styled the joint up with some effortless runs. Their familiarity with the regional resource was expected, but still enviable.

Diego Cadena, another ripper from Sayulita, chimed in. "This is a favorite strike for us. There's a handful of surfers, mostly from Tepic, who know what it takes to work. They're the only guys we really surf with up here."

The jungle track was only drivable for a portion of the way to Stoner's proper, and even that required four-wheel drive. We parked on the sand at Little Stoner's, where teet-high rights whipped along a natural jetty before mushing off into a *quebrada*. The crew was amped and out there in an instant. I had other bones to pick.

Rock-stepping my way north, out of sight of the surfers, I found my way blocked by a small rock tower: Hetzel's perch. Clambering up the toeholds, I reached the top and peered over. It was 3 foot and cracking perfectly into the cove. Flawless, really. Dozens of surfers were simply not there. They were at Saladita or El Anclote or Salina Cruz. They had been swept along with the current, down to Instagram dreams with better access, fewer bugs, and a more open swell window. Better spots all around, if one needs to be honest.

Walking back down the beach to Littles, I saw another vehicle come to a stop at a respectful distance from our post. Two surfers emerged to take in the scene. Those in the lineup offered welcoming gestures as they paddled back out from their rides. The visitors took in the view, enjoyed a smoke, and started up their car. I was surprised to see them pull a U-turn in the sand, away from the empty perfection just out of sight. For an instant, "Stoner's" was gone and Hetzel's jungle cove reeled off by its lonesome.

Two Dog Circus

Surrealismo in central Baja.

From *The Surfer's Journal*, Volume 9, Number 4, 2000

San Quintín sprawls along the highway, debauched and sour, merging with the neighboring *colonias* in a megastrip of roadside sprawl. Migrants pour in from Central America and the mainland with high hopes but nowhere to go but down. A lot of glue gets huffed here, and when travelers are robbed or gang-stomped, the area between Camalú and Punta Baja is where it happens.

In the past, the region was a laid-back zone of year-round overcast, empty reefs, and rich brant hunting and yellowtail fishing. Today, San Q can seem a desperate place.

Three years ago, hundreds of laborers and their families were denied payment by their *patrónes*, and the looting commenced. When the military regained control they found the rabble in local markets and restaurants, gorging on raw meat and fish offal, clicking in their mountain dialects. The town has had a dark vibration ever since.

Jorge and I blow through the city with the windows up against a nimbus of insecticide and farmed-out dust. I can't help but think of the town as some dreadful indicator of Alta California's two-class future.

The situation improves as we drop into the Valle El Rosario, seeing the sphinx-like mountain formation that marks the central plateau. The first boojum and cardon are spotted, and suddenly we're in the true desert. Past the buried-tire corral of Tres Enriques, we drive across the spring-fed *vado* fringed with blue palms at Cataviña and down still farther to the winter hunting grounds.

My companion has been weathering a teeth-gnashing divorce, and his monologue chews through nine hours of driving. If his tales weren't salted with humor and ribald speculation on his bachelor future, they would be intolerable in their lack of topical range. Regardless, we're both ready for some peace as he turns off the motor, perched on the dune overlooking the small bay. The engine diesels, choking up the stepped-on gas bought out of a drum at Santa Ynez.

The view into the cove is a letdown. Swimming Pool Point is pretty much gone. The sand hasn't recovered from the hurricane that came aground several years ago. Fat waves drag their way to shore, shapeless and slow. An osprey spirals up an invisible thermal stalking corvina, looking vigilant and bored all at once.

Inshore, the evening glow marquees the shanties of the shark fishermen's camp with halogen spot beams of sun, highlighting a white shrine on the hill above. A group of young men walk toward us, finally close enough for one to gesture and hiss, "Relax."

We toss them a greeting. It's a much younger crew than I remember, streetwise and urban looking. A cold-eyed young man in a bandana scratches invisible insect bites. He's muscled and lean. "No," I answer to the tall one, "we don't want to buy any abalone or weed. Enjoy the evening."

While fishermen would normally show a healthy curiosity where rig and gear are concerned, this lot makes an obvious effort to avert their eyes. They stride back to their camp.

As we erect our tent, we hear a vehicle coming over the rise. Headlamps sweep the dunes, and the truck rumbles to halt 10 yards away. Jorge stares at the dusty Land Cruiser with its stack of boards, aghast. His cursing echoes across the landscape. Livid, he mumbles to himself as he assembles the fold-out kitchen. "Forty miles of coast without a soul. Forty miles. Give me a goddamn break." After a tequila, his outrage cools to amusement.

The fellow surfers keep to themselves, busily off-loading their truck.

The next morning's quiet is broken by the two-stroke whine of the shark pangas, off to the Cedros channel. Our new neighbors, having changed the flat they hobbled in with, are loading a day kit for an assault on the next point up. They drive off, leaving their tents and camp stove.

We while away the day with sessions in the limp surf interspersed with reading and investigations of the dunes. A coyote trots by with a crab in her teeth, a string of drool yoyo-ing from her chin.

A few hours later, Jorge treads back to our tent after a hike. "You're going to want to see this." We walk to the north side of the headland. I take the binoculars and glass the beach until I find them. The Land Cruiser is buried to the pumpkin in a drift of talcum sand up at the next point. Their stick figures work silently with shovels. A half hour later, the truck rolls free. To return they must traverse a mile of wet beach with a rapidly encroaching tide. They seem to know they're in trouble, accelerating toward us across the flats. A small point of rocks blocks their approach. Through the twin circles of the binos I see the truck fall into a hole, its snout buried under an explosion of saltwater, loose gear and parts blowing into the sky. We hoot and dance in the dunes.

The driver crawls the rig up the sand, the vehicle coming to a rest. The rocks have blown out the sidewalls of the two left tires. The engine is swamped. Bands of whitewater move incrementally closer with each set. Not wishing to stack stupidity on stupidity by risking our truck, we watch. *Un milagro*. A small army of fishermen walks toward them from the shark camp. They push the truck to safety en masse, and the beast sputters to life.

That evening we offer them a sundown drink, playing dumb, regaling in their version before letting on that we'd watched the whole thing.

We make time to explore the shark camp the following morning. I notice graffiti sprayed on the plywood walls of one shack. "Punta Mu." The name is unknown to me, and I've been coming here for 25 years. I ask the first fisherman I see about the name. He lifts his chin to the point out front and to the adjacent points as well. "*Punta Mu, Punta Mu…todos Mu.*"

In the space between two shacks, Jorge sees a cross and asks the fisherman of its significance. He explains that a drunken man fell asleep with a space heater on. It ignited, burning him alive before anyone could help.

We climb the hill to the shrine and peer inside. For the most part it's standard issue. A framed print of the Virgin of Guadalupe. Some candles. Mounted on the block wall, though, is something extraordinary: a *borrego* with an extra set of horns sprouting from its forehead. No obvious forensic clues as to whether it is assemblage or aberration. We chalk it up to genetics and head back to pack our gear and clean the site.

On the road out we investigate False Point. The sand is perfect and west lines spin off, their lips Saran-thin and speckled with darting baitfish. As we continue the drive, it's apparent that every spot save the accursed Mu is rifling.

Dropping into the lee of the next point, we see it. Stark against the hardpan, flags snapping in the afternoon wind, a dusty blue big top is silhouetted against the glare. "Circo Andreau," the truck reads. The tent is staked to the ground with car axles, their hubs still attached. It out-Fellini's Federico himself. Driving through the adjacent fish camp we slow to interview a passing man about the circus. "It tours the camps," he tells us. "No matter how small. One man and his wife. He erects the tent and serves as ringmaster. She vends the tickets and is the clown."

He asks where we have come from. I mention the mapped name of the point. "Oh," he says. "*Muy malo. Mucha chiva. Muchos adictos.* They are sharkers. They trade the fish for heroin to their ice truck driver from Ensenada. They fish all day and do *chiva* all night. *Muy malo.* Did you see the cross? That is where they boarded in one of their own and burnt him alive. *Muy peligroso, ese lugar.*"

I ask him of the word itself.

"*Mu? Es Mu y nada más. Mu.*" He forks his fingers behind his head and bugs his eyes. "*Contrario a los dios. Mu.* Against the gods, my friend."

The man's little boy is standing on our running board, smiling and sucking on the candy I bring as baksheesh for such occasions. As his father walks away, he stays on the truck as we troll toward the main road. I ask if he has seen the circus.

"Three times," he says, grinning.

"What do they have at the *circo*?" I ask. "*Tigres? Leones?* What class of animals?"

"*No tigres. No leones.* Two dogs only." He jumps from the running board. I see him in the rearview mirror, chasing after us. Jorge slows down.

"*Solo dos perros,*" he screams in our dust. "*Dos perros solamente.*" He's laughing as he turns on his heel, marching back to the camp.

Acknowlegements

Every surfer, artist, and fisherman appearing in this volume was selected not just for their tradecraft, but because they are always welcome to my campfire. Beyond that, I'm indebted to the friends and colleagues who have urged things forward, being there for the offshores and, on grimmer days, the foul weather.

In no particular order: George Ravenscroft, Steve and Debbee Pezman (heck, their whole clan), Craig Roberto Stecyk III, Brandon Hayward, Tim Elsner, Jeff Kramer, Kevin Miller, Devon Howard, Mark Kronemeyer Coppel and Begonia Felix, Donald Takayama (DEP), Rodney McCoubrey, Jesús Salazar, Joel Tudor, Alex Webb Wilson, Jon House, Ira Opper, Barberia Don Edgar, Chris Lab (DEP), Jeff Divine, J Brother, Juan and Miguel Plaza, Peter Maguire, Bryan DiSalvatore (DEP), Thomas Campbell, Whitman Bedwell, Harry "Skip" Frye, Ewan Morrison, Takuji Masuda, Jim Newitt, Art Brewer (DEP), Mike Morgan, Geoff Ragatz, Sam Ryan, Club Waikiki in Lima, Jamie Brisick, Kem Nunn, Fernando at Caesars, Josh Farberow, Guy Motil, Tom Adler, David Holmes, Jonathan Steinberg, Mike Beeler, Matt Miller, John Durant.

This book was set in Genath, a serif typeface designed by François Rappo in 2011 for the type foundry Optimo. The design is based on a type Johann Wilhelm Haas created in 1720 for the Genath Foundry, which is where the typeface gets its name and is recognized as the most famous and oldest type foundry in Switzerland.